FOUND ATIONS OF**EXEC UTION**

YOUR**BULLSHIT-** FREE**GUIDE**TO **ACCOMPLISHING** ABSOLUTELY **ANYTHING**

BY **MATTHEW** CANNING

Foundations of Execution: Your Bullshit-Free Guide to Accomplishing Absolutely Anything
Copyright © 2019 by Matthew Canning
Edited by Lisa Picozzi
Published by The Influxa Media Group

ISBN 978-0-578-55189-0
First Edition: August 2019

MATTHEWCANNING.COM

FOUNDATIONSOFEXECUTION.COM

@MATTHEWCANNING

"This is for the lions living in the wiry broke-down frames of my friends' bodies."

—The Front Bottoms | "Twin Size Mattress"

CONTENTS

INTRODUCTION

Despite this book's title, I don't like the word *execution*, as people may be unfamiliar with its meaning. I grappled for some time with the idea of including the word *success* instead, but I dislike that word even more. Not only does it stink of the sort of superficial self-help nonsense found in the types of books you'd come across at checkout in an office supply store, but it's deceiving; it seems as though it should mean the same thing to everyone, but that couldn't be further from the truth.

To define *success*, you first need to identify exactly what you find valuable or desirable, and this varies wildly from individual to individual—it could mean freedom in one's career or the ability to help others; it could mean creative autonomy; it could mean fame and status; it could mean education, peace, or even something as bizarre as vengeance. I would call this desirable thing *wealth*, and an abundance of said wealth *success*; but *wealth* is itself deceiving in that, in popular usage, it implies only an abundance of money and possessions.

Your definitions of success or wealth may seem odd to others, and, likewise, it's likely you've seen others working tirelessly toward a definition of success or wealth you can't quite wrap your head around. But that's part of the intrinsic beauty of these ideas—other people don't need your approval to craft their definitions, just as you don't need theirs.

Regardless of your personal definition of success, we're all chronically overexposed to it. A little more than a century ago, if you wanted to engage with a massively successful individual, you'd have had a much more difficult time. Seeking out and securing the time and attention of someone who exemplified your definition of success would have required a huge amount of dedication; the business mogul, renowned artist, prodigious author, poet, actor, athlete, dancer, or spiritualist you admire was most likely not your next-door neighbor. Now, by contrast, many of our success models can be easily accessed online, their likeness digitized and cast into our homes in photorealistic 4K and available with the swipe of a thumb. This availability creates the impression that success is much more common than it really is, and therefore much more easily attained than it really is.

Couple this overexposure with the participation-trophy mentality bestowed on xennials and millennials, and we find ourselves in a position where almost no one born in the modern age could be faulted for operating with a palpable sense of success entitlement—or at least the impression that success, by any definition, was simply a product of hard work and time spent pursuing it.

For those of us who found out that hard work and time spent weren't enough, how do we realign our strategies? To whom can we turn for guidance?

The baby boomers provided an unrealistic model of prosperity, so their gurus' self-empowerment messages fall short in today's socioeconomic climate. To the younger among us, in fact, they often sound ridiculous, and as such, the value attributed to coddling mantras of positivity has plummeted. Believing in yourself isn't enough. Developing your character and working hard—harder than anyone else—may make you a stronger person, but it doesn't mean you're going to succeed. I've met plenty of miserable people with strong character. I've met plenty of hardworking unsuccessful people.

So, no matter how hard I tried to change the title, I kept coming back to *execution*; if your definition of success requires action on your part, it requires execution mastery—understanding and being able to implement tangible, repeatable behaviors that move you measurably closer to well-stated goals. It's the single most important set of skills you can acquire, and to understand why this is so, I urge you to think about your life as a series of stories. As a species, we speak in stories. Your life is a collection of stories that continue to be written; some of these stories may be inspirational and others tragic and cautionary, but before you begin writing any story that involves working toward a valuable goal or complex undertaking, it's important that you understand what *type* of story it is.

There are four basic narrative conflicts:

1. *Human against human*
2. *Human against nature*
3. *Human against society*
4. *Human against self*

When it comes to the stories that illustrate our struggle to achieve, accomplish, or overcome, we tend to think of them as *human against society*, *nature*, or *human*—external factors, hardships, and obstacles. In reality, these stories are of the *human against self* sort. Your primary obstacle is always going to be you, and this book was written in order to teach you how to overcome that obstacle.

This is the Shyamalanian twist in your story: The villain was the hero the whole time (gasp!).

I wrote this book for a simple reason: The saddest thing I see on a regular basis—to paraphrase an old adage often attributed to Henry David Thoreau—is people "going to their graves with their songs still inside them." I consistently meet individuals with brilliant ideas, ambitions, and dreams that could bring immense fulfillment to their lives or the lives of others, but who have no idea how to execute. I consistently meet individuals who have immense creative potential but relive cycles of mediocrity. I consistently meet individuals who have ideas that could change the world but who claim they'll *get around to it when the time is right*.

They'll most likely put their goals off until they're too old or too tired to begin.

Looking back, these individuals will think they failed due to weakness, bad luck, or failure of character; but the fact is *execution is a skill, and until this skill is learned and mastered, one's dreams will remain just that: dreams*. It's heart-wrenching, and if I can change that trajectory for even a few people, I'll have left the world a better place than I found it.

I've guided individuals through unique challenges across a wide range of domains. I've helped professionals craft their career paths and come up with actionable plans to execute on their long-term goals. I've helped business leaders find and refine their personal leadership styles, become intimate with their values, and systematize the processes that eat away at their time. Beyond business, I've used the same principles to help creatives break free from lives in which they've felt imprisoned, and individuals from all walks of life to escape cycles of personal failure. I've spent an immense amount of time interviewing individuals who consistently execute to find out what works for them, identify common themes, and derive from them repeatable behaviors. I know what works and what doesn't, what's a waste of time and what isn't, and which factors actually make a difference. Luck matters less than you think. Intelligence matters less than you think. Motivation and self-discipline are bullshit, and you should never rely on them to take you anywhere.

In this book, you're going to learn how to set goals and turn them into reality not through vague inspirational advice or even through the stories of others' successes, but rather by learning and mastering simple, practical behaviors that are universally applicable and will better prepare you for any complex challenge you face. These principles address the way you think, behave, and approach problems in a broad sense, and anyone who tells you it's possible to achieve great things without addressing these types of fundamental changes to *self* is setting you up to fail—either right out of the gate or years down the line when you find yourself waist-deep in complexity, responsibility, and stress without any idea how to handle it.

Look in the mirror and behold your greatest advocate and your greatest enemy. *Human against self.*

I don't want to *motivate you*; I want to *give you the tools you need to execute despite the lack of motivation* that will inevitably befall you. I don't want to *train you to abstain from excuses*; I want to *give you the tools to strip all power from the excuses* that will inevitably bubble to the forefront of your consciousness. I don't want to *argue the same tired case for self-discipline* and convince you to *work against your nature*; I want to *show you how to circumvent your nature* when it undermines your interests.

It's for these reasons that this book is far less about *success* than it is about *execution*—the ability to set a goal, devise a detailed plan to achieve it, and work through the steps of that plan until you do so—so I'll simply have to deal with the fact that some people will mistakenly think this book has something to do with electric chairs, lethal injection, and firing squads.

English is a pain in the ass. Hopefully the subtitle helps.

THE FOUNDATIONS OF EXECUTION

In my experience, there are three behaviors that typically separate those who consistently execute on their goals from those who consistently fail to do so.

Those who execute:

- Define and refine their intentions
- Manage complexity
- Remove failure from the equation

It almost sounds too simple to be true, but I promise you it is. Aside from the very lucky, the very well-connected, and those who have the financial resources to treat life like a giant experiment (failing repeatedly before finally figuring things out), these three behaviors, in most cases, comprise the delta between the ability and inability to execute. There are, of course, countless specific behaviors and habits that can help or cripple the ambitious, but these three are by far the most fundamental. By the end of this book, you'll have mastered all three.

I call these three behaviors the **Foundations of Execution**, and they live at the core of everything I teach—whether to individuals, leaders, or students—and they'll serve as the building blocks of everything you'll learn here. We'll address the three **Foundations of Execution** in order.

PERSONAL CULTURE

Before continuing, I'd like to define something I call **Personal Culture**. It provides a simple way to articulate the necessary fundamental changes to *self* I mentioned earlier.

To begin, what's a *Culture*, in general terms? At its core, a **Culture**—of any sort—is defined by:

- **Values**: The things you feel are important
- **Behaviors**: The things you do and the way you act
- **Traditions**: Actions and stories that paint a picture of your **Values**
- **Language**: The terms or symbols you use that are unique to your **Culture**

You're likely part of multiple **Cultures**—friends, clubs, neighborhoods, professional circles, and families each have their own respective **Cultures**. Along with these, you're also part of a **Personal Culture**—one that begins and ends with *you*. Within your **Personal Culture**, you and you alone define which **Behaviors** are celebrated and which aren't tolerated—the way you communicate, what you eat, how you dress, the things that define you, and the impression you make on others. Throughout the course of this book, we're going to make constant references to the **Values**, **Behaviors**, **Traditions**, and **Language** that comprise your **Personal Culture**, and you're going to be asked to refine your **Personal Culture** quite a bit.

If you think about it, you're already altering and building on your **Personal Culture**. By getting ahold of a copy of this book and dedicating time to reading it, you've already demonstrated something about your **Values**. In the coming pages, I'm going to ask you to send an email or text to a friend or family member; this is a **Behavior**. The term **Personal Culture** is now part of your **Language**, and by the end of this book, you'll have an entirely new **Language** with which to talk about your goals and the ways in which you operate. Lastly, you'll come away with several new things you'll do every day; those are **Traditions**.

A QUICK EXERCISE TO GET STARTED

Before beginning, there are two small things I'd like you to do—consider them insurance policies.

First, answer the question: *When do you plan on working on the content found in this book?*

When doesn't mean "I'll dedicate an hour today, and another on Wednesday, if I can, and take it from there." *When* means committing to an actual schedule: *what days*, *what start times*, and *what durations?* Yes, you're busy, but if you're reading this, you either want to execute on some specific goals or believe in the overarching value this book's message could provide you, so you need to dedicate the time necessary to make progress. I'm willing to bet you can commit—for example—a half-hour twice each week to this book beyond any time you already planned to dedicate. Think of the ways you spend your time; can you forgo a certain TV show? Can you wake up a half-hour earlier on Sundays? Is the final waking half-hour on Wednesday night really that productive (and would your browser history support your answer)?

Committing specific times to a task and engaging with it on a schedule helps ensure you'll remain consistent when your situation changes—and it will. You may be inspired right now, but will that still be the case a week from now? You may have some free time right now, but will your schedule be the same next month? *Fitting it in when you can* is a recipe for failure. You probably already know this, but knowing is easy; I'm asking you to act.

Consult your calendar, your spouse, your work schedule, your Magic 8-Ball—whatever you need to do—and refine your *when?* answer. Before moving on, settle on at least two half-hour sessions per week you can dedicate to this book. We'll refer to these sessions as **Blocked Time**.

Once you've done this, here are the ground rules for each session:

1. No exceptions
2. No distractions

No exceptions: While you can certainly pick this book up more often (the more, the better), consider these two sessions of **Blocked Time** non-negotiable unless you're being seen in an emergency room for a crossbow injury or actively dealing with a house fire. Beyond that, these times are off-limits. If you're simply hanging out in the ER waiting room with an arrow in your shoulder or standing safely curbside post-fire, don't make excuses.

You aren't sure if I'm joking or not. I'll leave that up to you.

No distractions: This means no checking your phone or email. It means making sure your pets are fed beforehand. It means ignoring that call from mom. Respect the time slots you just allocated, and just as importantly, socialize that respect: tell your spouse, your kids, your parents, your roommates, or your boss if you're working through this book at your job. Tell them—unless there's a true emergency—to leave you the hell alone until your **Blocked Time** has ended.

This is the first thing I want you to internalize: If you don't have specific times dedicated to this book (and standards for those times), your chances of giving up go through the roof. Make a plan.

Next, send a text or email to someone you trust with some version of the following:

> *Hey there,*
>
> *I'm reading a book that's really important to me, and I want to make sure I follow through without giving up. Can you set a reminder for yourself to text or email me every Friday to check in on me and make sure I'm still doing it? If I'm slacking off, give me a hard time and tell all our friends what an awful loser I am. Thanks, I owe you.*
>
> *Sincerely,*
> *Me*

Stop here until you're done sending this to someone. It doesn't matter if you think it's cheesy; don't skip this.

I'll wait.

Accountability does wonders. Sending this simple message will make it less likely that you'll give up when you become busy or tired or face challenges during your journey through this book—and I promise you all three will occur at some point. Much like the **Blocked Time** mentioned above, you most likely already know this works, but I'm willing to bet you fail to leverage **Accountability** with any structure or regularity. Some people fail to do so because of laziness, others because of pride, and still others because they've simply never been in the habit of doing so.

Again, knowing is easy. It's time for action.

Later in this book, we're going to take some **Accountability** principles and build on them in unique ways that will leverage your own psychology to reduce (or, in many cases, completely eliminate) the risk of inaction or failure. This simple little note to a friend or loved one is a great introduction to this mindset.

Are you excited? I'm excited. Let's begin.

THE FIRST FOUNDATION OF EXECUTION: DEFINE AND REFINE YOUR INTENTIONS

Those who consistently execute operate with a level of **Intentionality** often overlooked by others. In this context, **Intentionality** simply means performing a task or tasks with purpose (as opposed to just *performing them*). Ben Franklin famously asked himself, *What good shall I do this day?* each morning, and *What good have I done today?* each evening. While even such a simple and loose demonstration of **Intentionality** will provide value, you're going to take a much more robust approach.

The best way to embrace **Intentionality** is to define and refine your intentions, and in order to do so properly, you need to understand your goals at two different scales—how they relate to larger, overarching, life-spanning **Values** or motivations, and in a more granular, actionable, goal-specific sense. In doing so, you'll set yourself up for success in ways you may have never imagined possible. If you began reading this book with a specific goal in mind—something around which you'd like to achieve success by whatever metric you use to define it—I'm afraid you most likely don't have a goal yet. You have a **Dream**. A **Dream** is ambiguous and lacks clear criteria for achievement or a plan of action; it isn't truly a goal until you've reinforced it with all of the necessary execution attributes.

At its simplest, the mission of this section is to turn **Dreams** into goals.

DEFINE YOUR INTENTIONS

Before trying to refine any specific goals, you need to first become intimate with your overarching, life-spanning **Values** and motivations, as doing so will help you to articulate why success matters. Overwhelmingly, those who struggle or fail to consistently execute fail to do this.

Foundational Wealth

As mentioned in the introduction, people often associate *wealth* with money and possessions, but wealth is much more accurately defined as the leverage or power to consistently experience the type of existence you prefer. Money and possessions have come to be associated with wealth because—among other reasons—money is often necessary to participate in the types of activities many people assume they want to experience (leisure and luxury), and possessions are often indicative of a surplus of said money.

However, it could be easily argued that a practicing Buddhist or ascetic could consider themselves enormously wealthy/successful without any money or possessions whatsoever. To highlight this distinction, I like to use the terms *Foundational* **Wealth** and *Foundational* **Success** instead. I define **Foundational Wealth** (in pseudo-economics terms) as the currency you value at the deepest level, and **Foundational Success** as having a strong equity position in said currency. If you're honest with yourself about your personal definitions of **Foundational Wealth**, you can more precisely and consistently trace your motivations to their deeper roots. This will help you to better understand your goals and decisions, and make intentional choices that serve those motivations. This exploration can be both immensely valuable and profoundly humbling.

What's your definition of **Foundational Wealth**? Most don't tend to think about this too often or too deeply, so it can be difficult to get started. For many, the hardest part is being completely honest with yourself and shedding any concerns about how you may be perceived. Free yourself from this burden up front; as you explore this question, do so knowing that you and you alone will hear the answers. Here are some questions to help prime your reflection:

- Of what accomplishments are you most proud? Why?
- Of what attributes, traits, or characteristics are you most proud? Why?
- How do you want to be remembered? Why?
- What are you doing at your happiest?
- If you could affect or help two groups of people, who would they be? Why? (Interpret *groups* in any way you'd like.)
- What would you do if you never had to earn money again? Why?
- Who is dependent on you, and in what contexts? What do you like and dislike about the nature of that relationship?
- To whom (or what) do you currently have to answer? To whom are you accountable?
- What did you want to do when you were five? Ten? Seventeen? Do you still feel a connection with those desires, forged from a more innocent mindset?
- Think of individuals you admire; what about their lives, ideals, or careers do you see as worthy of admiration? What do you think **Foundational Wealth** might mean to those individuals?

Think about these questions on the scale of your entire life and being, and answer them without any goals in mind. First, write your answers down quickly and associatively. Don't overthink them; just write what comes naturally. Then, go back and take your time. Labor over each question and try to dig into why you answered each question the way you did.

From your answers, I encourage you to craft two related definitions of **Foundational Wealth**:

1. An intensely personal, self-focused definition
2. An externally focused definition that centers around your effect on society

The first should essentially be selfish. It should seek to furnish you with aspects of the life you imagined when answering questions like, *What are you doing at your happiest?*, and *What would you do if you never had to earn money again?*

I've asked myself these questions many times over the course of my adult life and have come to recognize (and—over time—refine) what I value. To illustrate this concept, I'll share an aspect of my personal definition of **Foundational Wealth**: While I value many of the same things many individuals my age tend to value (quality time with family, career challenges and fulfillment, etc.), I felt those answers came too easily and challenged myself to articulate more precisely what's *novel* about the things I value—to identify the common threads among them and explore them more deeply. After a good deal of reflection, I concluded that my personal definition of **Foundational Wealth** revolves in many ways around *diversity of experience.* Life is short, I'm a high-energy individual, and I think consistency, relaxation, and routine are overrated. I love to travel, experience new things, gain insight into others' perspectives, meet new people, learn, and push the boundaries of my comfort zone. Whenever I'm experiencing something new, I succumb to a childlike sense of excitement and feel as though time slows to a crawl. I feel better able to focus on the present.

It was a major realization: Whether or not I was consciously aware of it, this simple idea has been a huge motivator throughout my entire adult life and has directly informed my risk tolerance. As I reflected on my past, I was reminded of example after example of professional, financial, personal, or lifestyle goals, and realized how *diversity of experience* (either immediate or deferred) has been the primary currency in which I've framed decisions and the potential for decisions to provide me with personal value. I came to understand that *diversity of experience* serves as a connective force between seemingly disparate motivations. I love experiencing new things with my family and feel as though I learn something new and unexpected about them every time we find ourselves somewhere unfamiliar. I also love experiencing new career challenges and relish the discomfort and growth that accompany them.

To summarize: When I'm regularly involved in *diverse experiences*, I consider myself *wealthy* by my self-focused definition. As much work as it was to come to this realization, it was profoundly impactful and connected many dots for me. I now keep my personal definition of **Foundational Wealth** actively in mind as I make decisions and refine goals.

The second definition of **Foundational Wealth**—centered around your effect on society—should describe ways in which you'd like to contribute to a larger purpose. It should seek to furnish you with aspects of the life you imagined when answering questions like, *Of what accomplishments or characteristics are you most proud?*, *How do you want to be remembered?*, and *If you could affect or help two groups of people, who would they be?* Note that I used the terms *your effect on society* instead of *your value to society* and *contribute to a larger purpose* instead of *contribute to the greater good*; while most people's definitions will naturally gravitate toward positive, society-benefiting **Behaviors**—and while I certainly encourage you to consider the greater good when crafting this definition—your definitions of **Foundational Wealth** are intensely personal, so I want to be careful about limiting them with that wording.

To again illustrate this with a personal example: I think daily about how the next Elon Musk, Salman Khan, and Oscar Wilde may out there in the world right now and could very well go to their graves never having shared their vision simply because they didn't know what to do. Whenever my insight and experience can help someone execute on the things they believe they were meant to share with the world, I consider myself *wealthy* by my externally focused definition. My being consciously aware of this definition drives me to work hard and continue sharing my message (hence, this book).

If you only have a self-focused, personal definition of **Foundational Wealth**, I urge you to think of ways in which you can affect others; you'll likely find that expanding your scope of influence enriches your self-focused definition and brings you increased fulfillment. On the other hand, if you only have an externally focused definition of **Foundational Wealth**, I urge you to identify self-focused things you value; you'll likely find that you can engineer the former in order to achieve the latter. Referring back to my personal examples: While my self- and externally focused definitions of **Foundational Wealth** may seem unrelated on the surface, the work I've done and the decisions I've made in pursuit of my externally focused definition have furnished me with a staggering number of diverse experiences otherwise unattainable.

Stop here and spend some time reflecting on your own definitions of **Foundational Wealth**. This can take quite a while, but you need to do it before moving on. Dedicate sessions of **Blocked Time** to this endeavor. Once you're confident that you've come to understand them, write them down and keep them in mind as you explore the strategies you'll use to further define and refine your goal.

CMV

It's time to talk about actual goals. You're going to learn a unique approach that ensures your intentions are well-defined by looking at them from three separate perspectives. I call this **CMV**.

CMV stands for **Credo**, **Mission**, and **Vision**. These are terms you may have heard associated with businesses or brands, but they're valuable tools for professional, personal, and creative goals, as well.

Here's a breakdown:

Credo

- Beliefs about what's valuable, important, or desirable
- A Latin word that means *a set of fundamental beliefs or a guiding principle*
- Begins with "I believe…"
- Example: *I believe that individuals in malaria-ridden countries should have the opportunity to live long, healthy lives.*
- While it doesn't necessarily call your definitions of **Foundational Wealth** out directly, your **Credo** should align with them

Mission

- Your purpose or calling
- Begins with "To…"
- Example: *To increase malaria vaccination availability in third world countries*

Note that your **Mission** is an actionable manifestation of your **Credo**, which is itself guided by your definitions of **Foundational Wealth**. Everything flows together.

Vision

- An image of the **Mission** accomplished (or being accomplished)
- An ideal future state (framed within the scope of your influence)—though not necessarily an *end* state—which would be possible only if your **Mission** was successful
- Reflects high standards
- Creates a visual scene
- Worded in the present progressive ("it is") or present perfect progressive ("it has been") tense

- Example: *The cities and towns of historically malaria-ridden areas are bustling with healthy humans; when doctors encounter a case of malaria, they're genuinely alarmed and puzzled because it's so rare an occurrence.*

You can (and should) develop a **CMV** for every remotely complex goal or undertaking in your life that you value. The exact same structure can be applied to anything from cutting carbs or managing social anxiety to building a business empire. A **CMV**:

- Brings everything you do into focus and lets you make progress toward your goal with **Intentionality**
- Ensures you have a quickly accessible and simple way to illustrate your intentions, motivations, and purpose to others
- Helps inform decisions and risk tolerance
- Reminds you what to value/prioritize vs. what to disregard
- Sparks insight and provides guidance when you're unsure about your next step
- Keeps you more intimately engaged with your goal and therefore less likely to give up when things become difficult

While your definitions of **Foundational Wealth** should be all-encompassing and big-picture, applicable to multiple aspects of your life and decisions—and while **CMVs** should be built within the boundaries and **Values** your **Foundational Wealth** provides—I'm not suggesting you make a **CMV** for your life *as a whole*; instead, you should craft unique **CMVs** for every individual valuable and complex goal, undertaking, or project.

To continue with personal examples, here's my **CMV** for being a dad, which is easily one of the most valuable and complex things I've ever done. I created this years ago when my first child was born.

- **Credo**: *I believe a present, engaged, supportive, and encouraging adult model is critical to the development of wise, confident children.*
- **Mission**: *To instill in my children a **Culture** of curiosity and a passion for pursuing the things they value*
- **Vision**: *I meet my kids for dinner in 20 years and am reminded that they've grown to become individuals I admire and genuinely enjoy being with*

Think of how these three statements could inform my decisions, conversations, **Language**, **Traditions**, and **Behaviors**.

From my **Credo**, the phrase "a present and engaged adult model" reminds me to remain truly in the moment and resist the urge to engage with unrelated thoughts or actions when I'm spending time with my children. As an example, the nature of my career can sometimes make work/life separation a challenge (which is something I generally don't mind, since I enjoy what I do)—but I sometimes need a reminder to put my phone away.

From my **Mission**, the term "a **Culture** of curiosity" informs how I answer questions—I have the choice of answering my children's more complex questions dismissively or by showing that I value their curiosity and rewarding them with encouragement and by matching their enthusiasm. When my daughter asked me how a car engine worked at age four, I would have been justified in saying, "Look, this is going to go *way* over your head, so let's revisit it in a few years." Instead, I gave her a detailed yet age-appropriate version of the real answer, and then we spent some time that night building moving engine parts out of Legos. She most likely didn't follow everything we discussed, but she certainly enjoyed it and grew from the exploration process.

From my **Vision**, the phrase "individuals I admire" reminds me to instill in my children the values and attributes I see in people *I* admire—to teach them about integrity and to encourage them to question authority but recognize when someone is looking out for their best interests; to reward humor and encourage their interests so they become worldly, interesting, happy, and open-minded adults.

This **CMV** is guided by and complies with my definitions of **Foundational Wealth**. I value *diversity of experience* (my self-focused definition), and my **CMV** encourages me to seek out diverse experiences with my children, where I can engage with them in novel ways, furnish them with opportunities to exercise curiosity and passion, and help them cultivate the breadth of experience needed to become worldly and open-minded. I want to consistently *help them achieve the things they value* (my externally focused definition) by empowering them to seek out whatever it is that *they* see as **Foundational Wealth**, even if it's drastically different from my own definition.

While **Credos**, **Missions**, and **Visions** are all valuable and should be used to inform almost every aspect of a goal, in many cases, **Credos** and **Visions** can be kept close—but **Missions** should be shared with the widest appropriate audience. This is true in almost any context. For intensely personal goals, the widest appropriate audience may just be *you*—and that's perfectly fine—for other goals, though, it may be friends, family, coworkers, and anyone you've asked to hold you accountable. For larger goals, the widest appropriate audience may include many more people.

To close with yet another personal example, consider a **CMV** I crafted for myself in a technology leadership role I had. While I only shared my **Credo** and **Vision** with a few of the key leaders who reported to me, I shared my **Mission** far and wide. It sat at the top of nearly every piece of documentation I created, it was laminated and posted on my office door, and it adorned the back of my computer monitor, so anyone sitting across the desk from me could read it without even having to turn their head. After some time, I began to hear members of the team citing it in conversation or when making critical decisions.

The **Mission** was: *To utilize my experience to develop one of the greatest software engineering teams in the company—a team whose expertise will* *be admired, whose processes will be emulated, and whose guidance will be sought.* Think of how that may have informed my pursuing growth or visibility opportunities for my staff; how that may have informed my willingness to have tough conversations or address underperformance; or how that may have influenced the care I put into developing robust, repeatable processes.

This also reflects my definitions of **Foundational Wealth**. I wanted to furnish my staff with opportunities to grow and—by encouraging them to adopt new ways of doing things and share their expertise outside their immediate teams—to *experience new things* and *push the boundaries of their comfort zones* (my self-focused definition). I also wanted to invest time and energy in understanding my staff members' individual motivations and *help them achieve the things they value* (my externally focused definition).

There you have it. Understand what truly drives you, and use that knowledge as a guide for creating **CMVs** for anything complex or valuable you pursue. Before moving on, spend some time crafting **CMVs** for any current goals that meet these criteria.

REFINE YOUR INTENTIONS

Any goals for which you've crafted a **CMV** are now dripping with **Intentionality**. Great work. However, they're most likely not *really* goals—at least not yet; they're still in **Dream** territory. To make them true goals, you're going to have to add quite a bit more detail.

You're going to do this by learning about **M-SMART Goals**.

M-SMART Goals

Learn Spanish isn't really a goal because you don't have any criteria by which you can say you achieved it. Almost everyone in the United States, South and Central America, and Europe technically speaks *some* Spanish—most people have probably said or at least heard the word "adios." Furthermore, even highly educated native Spanish speakers realistically speak only part of the language; I doubt many people know every single Spanish word, much like you and I don't know every single English word. *Knowing* a language isn't really a black or white thing.

So, at what point can you say you *"learned* Spanish?"

Does knowing how to say, "¿Dónde está la biblioteca?" count as having learned Spanish? Or is that not enough? How about being able to watch a Spanish-language soap opera and follow along with the plot? Or being able to hold a conversation in Spanish with a native speaker without their knowing it wasn't your first language? That one may be a bit unrealistic.

With this ambiguity highlighted, what are the criteria by which you'd be able to say you've achieved your goal? This is my point: it's important to *refine* goals you value—to add details about your execution plan, timelines, and desired end result.

Plain Old SMART Goals

I feel a little dirty discussing **SMART Goals** because they've been addressed *ad nauseam* by thousands of personal development educators and corporate trainers. Along with words like *synergy*, it reeks of the type of overused business jargon that makes you want to pair the word with an air quote gesture. Buzz-term or not, they're an incredibly simple and effective way to think about goals.

If you're not familiar, a **SMART Goal** refers to a goal that's specific, measurable, attainable, realistic, and time-bound.

To illustrate, let's turn *learn Spanish* into a **SMART Goal**: *Be able to speak Spanish well enough to watch and understand all dialogue in the film* Die Hard *in Spanish (without subtitles) on or before February 1, four years from now.* This is a purposely silly example, but it's memorable and perfectly illustrates **SMART Goals** and all they entail.

- It's *specific* — You chose to specify *"Die Hard"* instead of saying *"an action movie"* and *"Spanish"* instead of *"a foreign language."*
- It's *measurable* — In the big picture, you can measure success by whether or not you understand all dialogue by your deadline; if a single sentence evades you, you haven't succeeded. In the short term—that is to say, during the *process* of achieving your goal—you could quantifiably measure your improvement each time you watch the film; for instance, you could dedicate time to learning Spanish every Monday through Thursday, and then watch the movie each Friday; you could then write a plus or minus symbol on a piece of paper after each sentence of dialogue to signify whether or not you understood it, and then go back afterward and determine what percentage you understood, tracking your progress week over week. It's certainly a clumsy solution, but it makes the goal *measurable*.

- It's *attainable* — Human beings can learn new languages at any point in their lives. Others have done it. The goal isn't *to be the first person to speak Spanish on Jupiter.*

- It's *realistic* — The due date is set four years into the future, which—some cursory research will show—is an ambitious but reasonable amount of time for an adult English-speaker to learn a Romance language somewhat well. You didn't say you wanted to accomplish the goal *within three months.* Don't confuse *attainable* and *realistic*; *attainable* means *it can be done*, and *realistic* means *you* can do it within the time limits and constraints described.

- Lastly, it's *time-bound* — *Time-bound* and *realistic* are closely related. An end date is set, and it's expected that the goal will be reached on or before this date. You didn't say you'd learn Spanish *eventually.* There's an art to giving your goal's timeline some breathing room while not providing so much that you can afford to slack. Everyone has to take a break now and then, and life occasionally throws unexpected challenges your way. Later, you'll assign consequences to inaction and failure, so resist the urge to be hyper-aggressive when deciding on timelines. You'll also soon learn why the date you choose here will most likely not end up being your final deadline; rather, it provides an estimate that serves to guide your overall intention.

Executor Insight

"Have a deadline. If I have deadlines for projects, I get them done. If I don't have deadlines, I rarely make progress."

—Mignon Fogarty, a.k.a. The Grammar Girl
English/Grammar Communicator | Interviewed in 2013

We're used to ill-refined goals; they're baked into our **Culture's Language**. I constantly hear educated adults state their so-called goals with the same dismissive simplicity they probably exhibited when their fourth-grade teacher asked them what they wanted to be when they grew up. "Start a helicopter piloting school" is an ill-refined goal. "Create an iPhone app that helps identify wild birds" or "become the number one private wealth advisor in the region" are only a little better. What are three primary functions the wild bird app should provide? You want to become the number one private wealth advisor in the region by what metric? Customer satisfaction? Revenue? Market share? By when?

Take a few moments and construct **SMART Goals** from the following incomplete goals:

1. Be able to run a 5k
2. Learn self-defense

Take your time and perform some basic research, if necessary.

There are obviously many possible **SMART Goals** that could be extracted from these two incomplete ones, but here are some possible solutions for example's sake:

1. Be able to run a 5k in twenty-three minutes (under normal weather conditions) by this time next year.
2. Achieve a non-beginner degree in a self-defense-applicable martial art (such as blue belt in Brazilian Jiu Jitsu or green belt in Krav Maga) at a respected academy within two years.

Take a close look at these two **SMART Goals**. I think you'll agree they're both *specific, measurable, achievable, realistic*, and *time-bound*. Your research should have shown that if you aren't incredibly young or elderly and don't have any outstanding health or physical impediments, both running a twenty-three minute 5k and earning a non-white martial arts belt are realistic (though ambitious) in the respective amounts of time allocated.

Adding the "M"

Now let's talk about a *Foundations of Execution*-specific addition to the classic **SMART Goal**. As you may have guessed given all of the energy dedicated to **Foundational Wealth** and **CMVs**, the M stands for *Motivation*. An **M-SMART Goal** is <u>m</u>otivation-focused, <u>s</u>pecific, <u>m</u>easurable, <u>a</u>ttainable, <u>r</u>ealistic, and <u>t</u>ime-bound. As much as possible, your M should embody a concise summary of how the goal will help you realize your **CMV**.

While a **SMART Goal** may be formatted as *I want to achieve [goal detail] by [date]*, an **M-SMART Goal** would look more like *I want to achieve [goal detail] by [date] because [motivation]*. This will often result in a run-on sentence, a series of sentences questionably tied together with semicolons, or something of the like. That's okay; your high school English teachers won't see it. In many ways, the *SMART* aspects of these goals define paths to execution and reflect their respective **Missions**, while the M tends to speak more to **Credos** and **Visions**.

Here are two examples:

I want to build a marketing strategy consulting business with at least four active simultaneous clients and monthly revenue of over $1,000 on or before December 31st of next year because I enjoy working in the marketing field but feel that my vision, experience, and unorthodox ideas are underappreciated by my current employer.

That was definitely a run-on sentence. Another:

I want to write a novel about a young woman whose confidence and luck improve drastically after being bitten by a wolf, only to later realize that the power of positive change was within her the entire time and that the bite had nothing to do with it. I want to have it written, edited by a third party, and pitched to at least one publisher before December 31st of next year. I've struggled with confidence in my own life, so I want to explore the idea of finding inner strength and share the story with others who may be experiencing similar confidence issues.

That one was a full-out paragraph. That's fine, but don't go crazy and write a manifesto; you should be able to (loosely) recite your **M-SMART Goal** from memory. As an exercise, take the above two **SMART Goal** examples (*be able to run a 5k* and *learn self-defense*), come up with imaginary motivations, and add *Ms* to them.

The Exploratory Phase

Large or ambitious goals generally require research, and to intelligently refine your intentions, you need to become extremely knowledgeable about the *universe* in which your goals live—the overall domain or industry in which they reside (past, present, and potential future), the economics involved, the logistics involved, and the challenges unique to your specific intentions.

For instance, let's say you wanted to start a photography business. Who are your competitors in the area? Where are they located? Is the market oversaturated? What can you offer that's special, novel, or desirable? What gap can you fill? You need to consider the climate and physical attributes of your area; will weddings and events become less frequent when cold weather hits? Beyond industry-specific considerations, you need to think about the complexity inherent in running a business, in general. When incorporating, would it make the most sense to open an LLC, an S Corp, or something else? For tax reasons, does it make sense to open it in your home state or elsewhere? The nature of business itself is incredibly involved and can introduce unexpected hurdles and expenses that cripple your progress. Will you need a separate bank account for the business? If so, what are the best options in your area for business banking? What are the minimum balances for such an account, and how do you plan to initially fund it? What are your state's laws surrounding *piercing the corporate veil*, taxable income, and writing off expenses? Will the nature of your business or the equipment you'll own require you to procure additional insurance? Will you need customer agreements and contracts? Service packages? Customer relationship management tools? A marketing and web presence? I could keep going, but you get the point—and that's only if you're already an experienced photographer. If this goal represented a career change, you may also have to research equipment, develop your skills, and more.

I call this broad discovery process the **Exploratory Phase** (another term for the **Language** of your **Personal Culture**). Every **Mission** is unique, so every **Exploratory Phase** will be unique, as well. To begin, brainstorm some questions and allocate some **Blocked Time** each week to begin researching and coming up with answers. As an example, imagine that you want to become a chef. Some good questions to ask and answer would be:

- How long do culinary school programs typically run?
- When are they offered?
- What do they typically cost? Are financing options available?
- Which are considered the best in the world? Why?
- Which are considered the best in your part of your country? Why?
- Are they difficult to get into?
- Do you need experience to get in? Do you need to pass an entrance exam?
- What are typical entry-level positions for newly graduated chefs like? What do they pay? What are the hours like?
- How long does it typically take before a new chef can begin moving up the chain? What does progress look like?
- What are common pitfalls and pain points for new chefs?
- Who are some of the best chefs in the world right now?
- Who are some of your favorite chefs (and why)? Have you ever eaten their food?

- What does success mean to you in relation to this goal?
- How large-scale is your goal? Do you imagine yourself happy in the kitchen forever, or do you plan on owning your own restaurant one day? If that's part of your goal, it expands the scope quite a bit and could result in a much more complex **Exploratory Phase**, additional steps and considerations, and longer timelines.
- Online culinary communities exist; what are the best ones for someone in your situation, and would it make sense to embed yourself in its dialogue, either as an active participant or a lurker?

Never rush an **Exploratory Phase**, as it lays the groundwork for proper trajectory. Take your time and capture plenty of notes. After producing your list of questions, performing the necessary research, and feeling as though you're sufficiently knowledgeable about what you're getting yourself into, adjust your **CMV** and **M-SMART Goal** as needed. From here, you'll be able to formulate a rough draft of a plan using the framework you'll explore next, in the second **Foundation of Execution**.

Beyond the obvious benefits, an **Exploratory Phase** should also force you to look at your goal in the big picture—making sure that you're accounting for the impact its pursuit and achievement could have on your lifestyle and relationships. Determine whether your goal would require you to disregard other things in order to give it the attention it requires; if so, what goes? It should clearly articulate personal financial considerations. Will you need accreditations, permits, or authority you don't currently have? Will you need to develop new skills or expand existing ones?

These last few points lead us into our next topic.

Building a Body of Work

In many cases, your goals' criterion for success may be clearly measurable; you simply need to turn them into **M-SMART Goals**. *Gain* *ten pounds of muscle. Build a treehouse. Start a recipe blog.* Even more complex entrepreneurial or creative goals may sometimes come with cut-and-dry success criteria. *Publish a romance novel with a major publishing house. Have an album released on a major record label. Quit my job and run a dog-grooming business full-time.* However, the more complex and multi-step the goal, the more likely you'll need to consider interim steps that may seem peripheral but ultimately serve your **Mission**.

Take the *Publish a romance novel with a major publishing house* example. Imagine that you were relatively inexperienced with writing, but turned this goal into an **M-SMART Goal** and broke it down into phases. After a well-researched **Exploratory Phase**, it might look something like this:

Phase 1: Conduct research

- Become familiar with how books are typically written and structured; understand Freytag's Pyramid
- Decide on and complete an online creative writing course
- Read a few short works by romance authors you admire for inspiration and guidance on voice and tone
- Become familiar with the economics of story writing; even if you aren't concerned about income from your work, understand the royalty and "advance" models for compensation
- Become familiar with the publishing process and how authors are typically discovered by publishers; understand the role of the literary agent in the process

Phase 2: Write a book

- Brainstorm ideas
- Create an outline
- Decide on voice, style, etc.

- Write
- Edit
- Step away from it for a bit and then edit it a second time

Phase 3: Have the book published

- Research how to write query letters
- Research literary agents who specialize in the romance genre; assemble a list of agents you'd like to work with
- Send query letters to agents; keep a running spreadsheet listing who was contacted, when, and if you received a response

While it can clearly be broken down into much more detail, the above is an example of a well-researched, well thought-out plan. But it's missing something. Note that at the end of this plan, you'll be sending query letters to agents; but who are you? I've got bad news for you: you're nobody. With pursuits like this one, it often makes sense to hone your craft and build some credibility first. There are many ways to do so. For example, after the *Conduct research* phase but before *Write a book*, you could take a detour from your novel-publishing goal to write some short stories in the same genre and try to have them published by online literary magazines. Doing so would serve several purposes:

- Writing a few short stories would give you practice in the art of writing, which can benefit the quality of your eventual novel. No matter how good you think you are, practice will make you better. Get beginner mistakes out of the way.
- You could get the opportunity to share your work with members of online writers' communities, which would be a great way to acquire feedback and support without sharing your final masterpiece with the public.
- Sending your work to online literary magazines will give you experience with the steps involved in preparing submissions, adjusting to feedback, and dealing with rejection.

- Having your work published—especially if multiple works through multiple outlets—builds credibility that can go a long way in having you and your novel taken seriously by the agents you'll eventually query.

The lesson here, which applies to anything you do, is to look at the big picture. Make sure it takes into consideration things like skill acquisition and credibility. There are very few shortcuts to success—ever. If you've recorded the best album in the world, you're still nobody. You need to develop and deploy a plan to record and release a few tracks, market them through social media channels, build your network, and generate some authentic anticipation. Maybe you think you have the endurance to climb Everest, but before you set out to try (and risk joining the many hundreds who have died doing so), consider climbing a few less-daunting mountains. Expose limitations and learn about unexpected challenges while less is at stake. Maybe you have the best invention idea in the world, but don't have any experience with industrial design or prototyping, let alone pitching products to potential licensing parties. Maybe you think you're ready for the next step in your career, but have you really acquired enough relevant experience? Have you had difficult conversations and solicited unbridled critical feedback from peers and supervisors about your shortcomings and growth opportunities?

I certainly don't want to use the term *pay your dues*—as that implies *hours spent*, which can often be squandered focusing on the wrong things—but it's important to recognize the need to cultivate the experience, wisdom, networks, and credibility required to properly position yourself to execute on your eventual goal. We'll call this process **Building a Body of Work**. You should take it seriously and—once you've learned the best ways to break your goals down and track them—you should ensure your **Building a Body of Work** steps are represented and given as much attention as your goals' core tasks.

I'm sure there's a part of you who—eager to execute on your goals and confident in your intelligence, resourcefulness, and adaptability—will be tempted time and time again to skip steps related to **Building a Body of Work**. If I was there with you right now, I'd stare intently into your eyes as I say the following:

1. Skipping your **Building a Body of Work** steps is a mistake.
2. *Your goal* isn't an exception.
3. *You're* not an exception.

Recognize and incorporate steps that will serve your goal, even if they aren't directly and obviously contributing to it. Be patient and open-minded, and think of your goal as a journey as opposed to a destination.

Fantastic job. I assume. I can't see you. Move on when you're ready.

THE SECOND FOUNDATION OF EXECUTION: MANAGE COMPLEXITY

Learning a new skill or volunteering for a cause you care about is harder than sitting on your ass and watching TV. Just like having the tough conversation and moving all your stuff out is harder than staying in a bad relationship. These actions are harder not just because they involve work or emotional strain, but also because they introduce *complexity* to your life—they introduce unknowns and potential problems, anxiety and the possibility of regret. There's complexity in the unfamiliar and the risky, and haven from complexity in familiar routines and paths well traversed.

With very few exceptions, anything ambitious introduces complexity to your life. Think about it: adopting a pet, starting a new workout routine, or even traveling to a new location all introduce some degree of newfound complexity. Whether or not they're enjoyable, fulfilling, or worthwhile, embarking on them is always more complex than the alternative.

What about starting a business, reconnecting with an estranged loved one, pursuing a new career, taking on a creative challenge, committing to a lifestyle change, or working toward a professional goal?

Complexity. Complexity. Complexity.

Unless you're a filthy, stinking cheater who jumped ahead in this book, you probably recall from the introduction that there are three **Behaviors** or **Foundations of Execution** that generally separate those who consistently execute from those who consistently fail.

The successful:

- Define and refine their intentions
- Manage complexity
- Remove failure from the equation

We've covered the first one. Now, it's time to learn how to manage complexity. You most likely never learned to manage complexity properly—it's simply not something we're taught—so you never learned to manage ambitious goals (which are inherently complex) properly. And yet, you've doubtlessly heard the same advice from gurus, loved ones, colleagues, and inspirational memes scattered across social media: get out there and begin working on your goals today. Unfortunately, this is no different than telling you to start building the walls of your dream home without first laying a foundation. As goals evolve and progress, tasks and responsibilities begin to pile up, and anyone who lacks a concrete framework for prioritizing and organizing them is going to quickly become overwhelmed.

The overwhelmed tend to suffer. And those who suffer—especially before seeing benefits—tend to quit.

Moreover, complexity doesn't emerge only from your ambitions, but from all aspects of your life—whether interesting or mundane—and you need to learn to manage complexity in all of its forms. Luckily, managing complexity doesn't have to be complex. You can build a framework that leverages basic organizational skills and simple technology. In exploring this second **Foundation of Execution**, we're going to ask and answer three questions:

- **How?** — *How* will you organize your goals?

- **When?** — *When* will you address your goals?
- **What?** — *What* tools will you use to record/represent your goals and the time you've committed to addressing them?

If you're reading this book with specific goals in mind, you're going to forget about them for a while and simply rewrite how you organize your tasks, time, and goals, in general. This may seem a little bit like homework in the beginning, and it may feel at times as though you're losing sight of your specific goals, but these changes to your **Personal Culture** lie at the core of everything you're going to learn. If you take this **Foundation** seriously—if you absorb it into your very soul and let it change how you operate on a fundamental level—you'll grow in ways you never thought imaginable.

Three simple questions. Let's address them one by one.

HOW?

There are hundreds—if not thousands—of suggestions for personal organizational processes out there. The topic has been explored for centuries, and in order to claim novelty status, systems are often made ridiculously complicated. What you'll find here is simple by contrast, but it's the only framework you'll find that scales perfectly from day-to-day tasks to large-scale goals. You can use it to jump-start a car battery or oversee a sizable technical organization at one of the world's largest companies.

That's not an exaggeration; I've done both.

You're about to learn how to create two resources for each thing you work on—every project, personal objective, and professional goal. We're going to call these resources a **Script** and a **Hot List** (two new terms for the **Language** of your **Personal Culture**), and they're going to be core to everything you do throughout the rest of this book.

Scripts

A **Script** is a simple, ordered, linear process that you follow to keep yourself on task whenever it's time to work on something. Your **Scripts** shouldn't change much from day to day—you won't be deleting or editing items (at least not often).

To illustrate this, imagine that you're a professional with an office job. You come into work in the morning and pull up your work **Script**:

1. Check your work email and voicemail and reply as needed
2. Assess any new items you need to keep track of and add them to your to-do list
3. Check your calendar; review the day's meetings and prepare notes for each

4. Perform daily repeated tasks
5. Address your to-do list

I call this type of **Script** a *Daily* **Script**. Once you arrive at work in the morning and get settled, you know it's time to refer to this **Script**; in **Personal Culture** terminology, it becomes a **Tradition**. A **Daily Script** can work for a job, a morning routine, or even as a way to provide structure upon retirement.

A **Script** like the one outlined here may seem insultingly obvious, but it exemplifies a habit I'm going to be reinforcing time and time again throughout this book—the habit of recording every remotely complex process you perform. I have dozens of multi-step processes I need to follow in all aspects of my life—some of which I only have to reference a few times each year. Do you think I want to have to remember every step of each? No—I don't want that burden or the stress that accompanies it. Personally, I've used **Scripts** for opening a pool, collecting materials for taxes, intonating a guitar, assembling children's school lunches, and dozens of other multi-step, repeated processes. Professionally, I've used **Scripts** for performance evaluations, root cause analyses, new staff onboarding, financial forecasts, process audits, training, technical security reviews, and more.

Note that the item *Perform daily repeated tasks* in the above example could refer to anything applicable to your specific job. Think of a job right now—either your current job or one you've had in the past. If you're in IT, you may need to review technical logs every morning; or maybe you're a retail manager who needs to look at the night shift's final tallies. Maybe you're a competitive athlete who performs visualization exercises before starting your daily training regimen. Maybe you're a contractor who needs to clean your tools and stock up on materials for the day. Do you change ink cartridges, check tire pressures, manage your stress with mindfulness practices, or feed all of the animals in a shelter? Do you order new inventory? Almost everyone has things they have to do or check every day, and there's value (and often safety) in organizing them and articulating them outside your head as opposed to relying on your memory, which can be affected by countless factors.

Creating a reliable, meticulously organized, and consistent ordered process for any multi-step task not only helps to reduce oversight, but also *the anxiety that often subconsciously accompanies the fear of oversight.*

"Shit—did I skip a step in opening the pool and damage my pump?"

"Shit—I feel like there was one more item I collected for my taxes last year. What was it?"

"Shit—this kid's lunchbox looks kind of empty. Am I missing something?"

Avoid the *shits*.

The examples given so far have focused on tasks and processes, but **Scripts** really shine when it comes to goals. Consider a personal goal: imagine that you're learning to juggle and set aside two dedicated thirty-minute practice sessions each week. What could a **Script** look like for each chunk of **Blocked Time**?

1. Locate your juggling materials (1 minute)
2. Set up in a quiet place; mute your phone (2 minutes)
3. Stretch (2 minutes)
4. Review fundamental exercises (5 minutes)
5. Review most recent exercises (15 minutes)
6. Study new exercises (5 minutes)

I know nothing about juggling, but I think that's probably a decent guess (and I'll wait for a professional juggler to correct me).

For some **Scripts**—especially those that relate to skill acquisition, like juggling—adding time limits to each item may make sense. In other cases—such as in the *Work* **Daily Script** above—you may simply want to work through each item until you've completed it. Use your judgment given the nature of the **Script**.

What would a **Script** look like for learning sign language or how to play guitar? Pick one of the two (or any practice-oriented discipline with which you're more familiar) and create a **Script** for it. What would you do consistently during each session? Remove as many decisions as possible from your workflow. *Mindless process* is the name of the game; imagine that these instructions were written for an understudy who lacks the context to make educated assumptions.

Once finished, look at the **Script** you just created and take a moment to consider what you're doing here; you're *outsourcing* a process from your brain to an external artifact. The steps you go through during each practice session for guitar or sign language may seem obvious, but in providing yourself with ordered instructions, you're assigning **Intentionality** to the time you spend working on it. It's becoming structured. It's becoming something you're taking seriously. This level of organization, applied to seemingly inconsequential processes like these, creates a shift in mentality that will prepare you for the complexity you're going to face when addressing much more complex goals.

Hot Lists

A **Hot List** is a simple, constantly changing, text-based list of prioritized tasks. It isn't just a *to-do list* (otherwise it would be *called* a *to-do list*). *To-do* implies items that—once addressed—can be removed, and that's not necessarily the case with **Hot List** items. While there may be *to-do*-style items on a **Hot List**, it may also contain items to which you need to continue paying ongoing attention.

Since we were introduced to **Scripts** through an office job example, let's do the same in order to become familiar with **Hot Lists**:

- Follow up with the legal team about the wording of the new advertising posters. *Last contact: Frank Doe (phone), 2/6, 5:39 p.m.*
- Talk to the recruiter about filling the sales position. *Last contact: Lara Gupta (email), 2/7, 3:11 p.m.*
- Schedule time with the boss to talk about next year's goals
- Get Dave White access to the new project management tool
- Schedule a meeting with the design team to discuss the new branding guidelines

A few things to note here:

First, the more important or pressing an item is, the higher it is placed on the list.

Next, you'll notice that certain items are nice and simple: *Get Dave White access to the new project management tool.* This is a classic *to-do list* item: you do it, it's done, you cross it off, and move on. However, not everything is like that. Some items require ongoing attention. Take a look at *Talk to the recruiter about filling the sales position* and note the comment at the end: *Last contact: Lara Gupta (email), 2/7, 3:11 p.m.*; this serves several purposes. First, if Lara claims you never contacted her about this topic, you can correct her, citing the day and time without second-guessing yourself or having to dig through your records. We communicate through multiple channels—in person, via email, over the phone, via text, or through messaging apps—so it's useful, in many cases, to note the channel through which the contact occurred so you have the option of quickly pursuing more detail should the need arise.

More importantly, recording the *last contact* gives you an idea about when you should follow up next; this makes it easy to stay on top of things and remain effortlessly responsible. To illustrate this, consider the first item, *Follow up with the legal team about the wording of the new advertising posters.* Note the *last contact* comment next to it.

Imagine that you and Frank from the legal team have gone back and forth several times about these posters, and now the ball's in his court—he has to make some changes and get them to you for review. Technically, at this point, you're absolved of responsibility; Frank is a grown man who's accountable for his own promises.

However, a simple note like this gives you the opportunity to showcase a heightened sense of ownership—to go above and beyond the call of duty. As you can see, your last contact with him was on February 6. When you come upon this item in your **Hot List** on February 7, you can say to yourself, "It's only been a day, so I won't bother him yet," and move on to the next item. The same can be said for February 8, February 9, etc. However, a week later, you may say, "You know, it's been a week, and I probably should have heard from Frank by now. I'll follow up to make sure he didn't lose track of this." You would then follow up and update the *last contact* comment. Updating the comment is simple, painless, takes only a moment, and removes a lot of ambiguity; you'll now know for a fact when your last contact was and can reference it almost immediately.

I can't tell you how many times over the course of my career and personal life I've heard, "Oh, I totally forgot about that—thanks for following up." Our lives and workplaces are awash in a sea of individuals for whom the volume and complexity of responsibilities have slowly grown over the course of years, and now find themselves drowning in a seemingly endless backlog and with no process with which to manage their workloads. Oversight, mistakes, and slippage have become the tolerable norm. However, amidst this chaos, here you are, cool and collected. This little trick can drastically change the way people perceive you, because it can make you seem more responsible and reliable—and that's not just *perception*; that's *reality*. That *is* you being more responsible and reliable. That *is* you staying on top of things. That *is* you inspiring trust. It just doesn't need to all be in your head—you can outsource the work and stress of remembering to follow up and have technology track it for you. You don't get an award for doing this without tools, and in the *What?*

section of this **Foundation of Execution**, you'll learn what tools are best suited for building and maintaining **Hot Lists**.

This isn't a wild, innovative secret, and yet almost everyone fails to take advantage of this type of simple **Behavior**. Those who struggle often assume the successful and organized are simply gifted and keeping all of their responsibilities in their heads; most of the time, that's simply not the case. I consider myself responsible and reliable—I pride myself on being so—and I can assure you my tasks, responsibilities, and commitments aren't all stored in my head. Far from it. I promise you that the dozens (sometimes hundreds) of *last contacts* I may need to reference in the coming weeks are captured digitally, and I'll be the first to admit that I'd be an absolute disaster if I wasn't employing these types of **Behaviors**.

You've already come to understand how **Scripts** can reduce the anxiety that often subconsciously accompanies the fear of oversight; the same is true for **Hot Lists**. If utilized properly, you no longer need to suffer from the uneasy feeling that you're forgetting something at work or home. The 2 a.m. realization that, "shit—I just realized I forgot to respond to so-and-so," or "shit—I never booked a rental car for the trip," or "shit—I just remembered I have to schedule bloodwork before the Tour de France" can become a thing of the past. This "shit reduction" is an important by-product of becoming organized that people often overlook. These **Behaviors** help battle one of the most pressing and constant sources of anxiety we face in the modern world: the shapeless weight of collected responsibilities.

If you were to suffer a blow to the head and become an amnesiac tonight, but have been following the processes you just learned, you should be able to look at your **Scripts** and **Hot Lists** after leaving the hospital and continue on with what you were doing without a single responsibility getting lost. And while amnesia is, of course, unlikely, consider that you can go on vacation for several weeks and come back knowing exactly where you left off relating to everything you were working on. I've also shared this process with employees who go on maternity leave or sabbatical. They hand off their **Hot List** to a peer with a little contextual explanation, and the delegate knows exactly what's already been done and what should happen next.

In order for this framework to be effective, however, you need to be diligent about truly recording every item that needs tracking and include enough detail to ensure that each is actionable. If you begin to miss things or let things slip, you're defeating the purpose, you'll lose faith in the process, and the whole system will go to hell. I'm personally diligent about my **Hot Lists** and prefer the negligible work of staying organized to the immense work and stress that accompanies inconsistency and failure. Any task or communication that requires action or follow-up—pretty much any worthwhile personal, professional, or creative task—is captured in an appropriate **Hot List**.

It can be strange to approach aspects of your life—your personal life, especially—with this level of organization, but I assure you that these are processes worth adopting and are non-invasive once you become used to them. And again, this will all translate from the day-to-day minutia you're learning about here to big goals like the one that brought you here. Simple **Behaviors** like this, repeated until they become habit, fundamentally change your **Personal Culture**.

Hierarchical Thought

You learned how **Hot Lists** can help you organize processes, multi-step tasks, and simple goals, but before you can apply **Hot Lists** to larger, more complex goals, you need to better understand how you handle information, in general.

Even as infants, we manage complexity by categorizing and placing things within hierarchies; it's a natural human tendency. The universe is comprised of objects, places, times, events, actions, and ideas that—while complex—relate to one another in consistent ways, and being able to use these relationships to predict future events and risks has immense evolutionary value.

This is so obvious and ingrained into the way we operate that it seems silly to think about (though doing so is the foundation of a serious field of study called *ontology*).

As a quick example of hierarchies, consider the following list of items:

- *John Wick*
- Incredibly irritating songs from the 1990s
- *Rambo*
- Rednex: "Cotton Eye Joe"
- Entertainment
- Films
- EMF: "Unbelievable"
- Music
- Action movies

Given only a few moments of sorting, you'd most likely be able to turn the above into the following hierarchy of nested items/lists:

- Entertainment
  - Films
    - Action movies
      - *John Wick*
      - *Rambo*
  - Music
    - Incredibly irritating songs from the 1990s
      - Rednex: "Cotton Eye Joe"
      - EMF: "Unbelievable"

Each item—other than the broadest—represents an instance or example of its immediate *parent* item (the one above it). Looked at another way, each item—other than the most detailed—describes its immediate *child* items (those below it). Once you begin to apply this somewhat obvious mental model more intentionally to increasingly larger and more multifaceted things, you'll begin to manage complexity in a more scalable and sustainable way that will serve you well when the time comes to tackle large-scale or long-term goals.

While an item may have multiple child items beneath it (for example, there are several films listed under the *Action Movies* item), an item can be associated with only *one* parent item (for example, *Coffee* couldn't be beneath both *Things I like* and *Things that are hot* without being duplicated). This is a limitation to two-dimensional mental models like this one, but it's an important benefit; this limitation will actually force you to keep things simple in a way that will prove useful.

To illustrate how you could apply this model in the real world, let's look at a fictitious person's entire personhood—a collection of her actions, how she spends her time, and the things she focuses on.

We'll call her Jackie. Like you, Jackie is dynamic and multidimensional, so she may choose to mentally organize her life such that the broadest practical distinction she can make separates her personal and professional interests.

- Personal
- Professional

She could then expand these top-level items to think of her life as a whole: The *catering business owner* Jackie; the *parent of three* Jackie; the *business student* Jackie; the *weekend acapella-techno DJ* Jackie.

- Personal
    - General to-do list
    - Parenting
    - School
    - DJ/Music
    - Health and fitness
- Professional
    - Work to-do list
    - Work meeting notes

- To-do list to prepare for upcoming vacation

However, Jackie doesn't always want to look at her life as a whole. She wants to be able to mentally "zoom in" on a distraction-free view of a single theme or specific undertaking—to compartmentalize. For example, drilling down within the *Health and fitness* item in the above structure should bring her to deeper items nested within it and push everything else out of view:

- Health and fitness
  - Soccer
  - Gym

Then, drilling down into the *Soccer* item should show her even further nested items:

- Soccer
  - Ball control drills to work on
  - Research stretching routine

We do this naturally, but it's useful to think about it intentionally because we'll be using this type of structure to organize more complex and large-scale undertakings.

With this mental model in mind, let's dig into **Hot Lists** a bit deeper.

Almost everything you'd ever want to accomplish, no matter how large or small, can fit under some sort of theme or heading. Embracing this approach—understanding where your goals fit within your life, as a whole—is key to managing complexity. Like Jackie, create separate **Hot Lists** for each such theme/heading in their appropriate place within an overarching hierarchy that loosely reflects your life. Examples of **Hot Lists** within a *Personal* list could be *Home improvement, Books I want to read, Things I want to learn,* or *Model airplanes to build.*

- Professional

- *General work* **Hot List**
- *Career growth* **Hot List**
- Personal
  - *Home improvement* **Hot List**
  - *Books I want to read* **Hot List**
  - *Things I want to learn* **Hot List**
  - *Model airplanes to build* **Hot List**

What about things that don't really fit into a project heading quite so cleanly? Something like *Scan old childhood photos* is unrelated to any project, so where would you place it? For these, a **Hot List** entitled *General personal **Hot List*** could work.

- Professional
  - *General work* **Hot List**
  - *Career growth* **Hot List**
- Personal
  - *General personal* **Hot List**
    - Scan old childhood photos
    - Look into helicopter lessons
    - Get tattoo of Nicholas Cage as his character in *Con Air*
  - *Home improvement* **Hot List**
  - *Books I want to read* **Hot List**
  - *Things I want to learn* **Hot List**
  - *Model airplanes to build* **Hot List**

You can then prioritize the items within that specific **Hot List** in relation to one another.

Handling Slightly Larger Goals

Even though they can seem intimidating, larger goals are really just comprised of a series of smaller tasks that share something in common. That sounds ridiculously, dismissively simple, but really think about it.

Both the Manhattan Project and Napoleon's plan for invading Russia were really just collections of a staggering number of individually actionable tasks that shared a **Mission** and were placed in a logical order.

Above, there's a *Things I want to learn* **Hot List** underneath the *Personal* theme. Imagine that it contained the following:

- Things I want to learn
    - Real estate investment
    - How to speak Brazilian Portuguese
    - How to snorkel

See the first item? *Real estate investment.* Imagine that you've always wanted to learn about real estate investment, but that isn't exactly a simple, cut-and-dry topic you can master in an afternoon. You can put aside time each week for this goal, but when those sessions of **Blocked Time** arrive, you may find yourself asking, "What do I actually *do*?"

First, you need to perform some research. Learn a little bit about the subject matter (remember: an **Exploratory Phase**), refine the goal, and decide on a series of smaller tasks that will culminate in your reaching the larger goal. When it comes time to work on this goal, you should follow a **Script**, which should eventually send you to your **Hot List**. An example of your *Real estate investment* goal in your *Things I want to learn* **Hot List** could, therefore, look like:

- Real estate investment
    - Read *Real Estate Investing for Dummies* (Eric Tyson and Robert S. Griswold)
    - Read *Property: Examples and Explanations* (Barlow Burke and Joseph Snoe)
    - Read about Internal Revenue Code 1031 (online)

By the time you actually begin working your way through this **Hot List**, you should be confident that it's well-researched, prioritized, and placed in a logical order; if so, you can focus on the first task (in this case, the first book you want to read). Once you finish the first task, you would know to move on to the second:

- Real estate investment
    - ~~Read *Real Estate Investing for Dummies* (Eric Tyson and Robert S. Griswold)~~
    - Read *Property: Examples and Explanations* (Barlow Burke and Joseph Snoe)
    - Read about Internal Revenue Code 1031 (online)

Think of this as though you were serving three roles in a small business dedicated to this goal: you act as the researcher, the project manager who organizes the goal and ensures progress is being made, and the individual performing the tasks.

Here, we've taken a goal—learning about a complex and multifaceted subject matter—and broken it down into several smaller, more manageable tasks (reading three books). We're going to call the larger task a **Major Task**, and the smaller tasks that comprise it **Minor Tasks**.

Let's explore a slightly more complex example: imagine that you need to plan your wedding, and this is the top item in your *General personal Hot List*. This is certainly a **Major Task**, because it isn't something that can simply be done all at once; it's comprised of many **Minor Tasks**. They include:

- Plan wedding
    - Select venue
    - Select date
    - Select theme
    - Invite guests
    - Select DJ
    - Get tuxedo (or dress)

Let's imagine that you've finished the first three **Minor Tasks** and need to begin the fourth, *Invite guests*. This is a **Minor Task**, because it's a component of the *Plan wedding* **Major Task**, but it doesn't tell you what actually needs to be done; it's not itself actionable. In reality, it involves several *even smaller* **Minor Tasks**, which can themselves involve even smaller **Minor Tasks**. As a result, there's no steadfast rule about what you'd consider a **Major** or **Minor Task** except in relation to its respective *parent* and *child* tasks. All but the highest- and lowest-level tasks are going to be *both* **Major** and **Minor**, depending on what level of detail you're focusing on. Let's expand the final three items under *Plan wedding*.

- Plan wedding
    - ~~Select venue~~
    - ~~Select date~~
    - ~~Select theme~~
    - Invite guests
        - Create an ideal, unedited list of prospective guests
        - Reduce the number of guests to comply with seating limitations
        - Locate contact information for all members of the final list
        - Purchase invitations, envelopes, and stamps
        - Address, stamp, and mail invitations
    - Select DJ
        - Research DJs online; make a list of prospects
        - Call each, interview them, confirm availability, and collect quotes
        - Decide on a DJ and book the engagement
    - Get tuxedo or dress
        - Research tux rental services or dress shops; make a list of prospects
        - Decide on one

- Go into the shop, get fitted, discuss details, and finalize order

If you think about it, this looks like the outline of a book: **Major Tasks** like *Select venue* and *Select date* are like sections, the first sets of **Minor Tasks** like chapters, and any deeper **Minor Tasks** like paragraph headings. While a **Hot List** can refer to even simple collections of tasks, when we're talking about a single goal broken down a few layers deep in this way, resulting in what amounts to an instruction manual for end-to-end execution, I call this a **Goal Scaffold**. You saw one of these already; when you learned about the **Exploratory Phase**, we used the example, *Publish a romance novel with a major publishing house*, and it was represented as a series of **Major** and **Minor Tasks**.

In many ways, we already do this in our heads all the time, even though we don't necessarily use this terminology or subscribe to the same level of detail. Think about it: isn't a grocery list simply an array of **Minor Tasks** that exist under the umbrella of the **Major Task**, *Go food shopping*? Organizing this way, you can break your grocery list down by store section, reducing any need to backtrack through the aisles.

- Go food shopping
  - Dairy
    - Milk (skim)
    - Almond Milk (vanilla, unsweetened)
    - Yogurts (Greek, raspberry)
    - Etc.
  - Fruits and veggies
    - Eggplant
    - Etc.

Sure, it may seem a little over the top to organize your grocery store list this methodically, but it's perfectly sensible to apply this model to more complex aspects of your life (like big goals).

As an exercise, break the **Major Task**, *Make a peanut butter and jelly sandwich*, into at least seven **Minor Tasks**. Imagine that this is a set of instructions not for you, but rather for someone who has never made any sort of sandwich before. The more detailed you can be, the less likely they'll be to miss a step or forget something.

Really do this. Take your time and continue when you're done.

How far did you break it down? How many layers? A *preparation/set-up* section, during which you check your bread, peanut butter, and jelly inventories, get everything out, and locate a knife and a plate? A *sandwich construction* section? A *clean-up* section?

Ask yourself if you could have broken things down further. This exercise may seem silly, but it serves to build a skill you'll need when it comes time to make sense of and tackle incredibly complex, daunting, multi-month or multi-year goals. Detail is your best friend.

With the PB&J example fresh in your mind, break down the **Major Task**, *Throw a birthday party for a five-year-old*, on your own however you see fit. Spend the time to organize it as clearly and logically as possible.

A Quick Note About Priorities

The order in which you need to execute on tasks is sometimes obvious. Consider the example of a screenplay's life cycle—*Brainstorm screenplay, Outline screenplay, Write screenplay, Edit screenplay*, and *Sell screenplay*. By nature, you don't really have too much flexibility in that order, as each **Major Task** has a dependency on the **Major Task** before it. In the same way, you would need to decide on the guest list for a wedding *before* sending the invitations. However, when it comes to independent tasks (such as *Paint the basement floor* and *Clean the shed*), an order may not be quite so obvious. Likewise, it can be difficult to prioritize unrelated tasks within a single goal when no dependencies are involved.

The best thing you can do to simplify prioritization is to build highly detailed hierarchies within your **Hot Lists** and **Goal Scaffolds**. If more than a dozen **Minor Tasks** exist within a single **Major Task**, consider whether the **Minor Tasks** share attributes that make them candidates for further grouping.

Imagine that you were an individual who was starting your own knife-sharpening business, and your **Hot List** looked something like this:

- Decide on company name (*Lookin' Sharp? Knife to See Ya?*)
- Sharpen the knives dropped off by Samantha G.
- Buy a new sharpening kit
- Take photos of recent work for website
- Sharpen the knives dropped off by Garrett T.
- Open a credit card in the business' name

You have six items competing for priority. However, if you refine it a bit, you may end up with:

- Company formation tasks
  - Decide on company name (*Lookin' Sharp? Knife to See Ya?*)
  - Take photos of recent work for website
  - Open a credit card in the business' name
- Current sharpening work
  - Sharpen the knives dropped off by Samantha G.
  - Sharpen the knives dropped off by Garrett T.
- General
  - Buy a new sharpening kit

This way, you now only have three **Major Tasks** competing for **Priority**, or which—in cases like this—can be treated like independent **Hot Lists** and addressed during different sessions of **Blocked Time** dedicated to each. Within each of these three **Major Tasks**, three or fewer **Minor**

Tasks compete for **Priority**. Organizing with this level of detail helps make prioritization simpler, but you still need to prioritize the most granular, actionable **Minor Tasks**: how do you decide whether to sharpen Samantha's or Garrett's knives first?

At its simplest, **Priority** is the recognition that some tasks need to be completed before others due to factors like deadlines, financial considerations, and risk. While you certainly shouldn't overthink **Priority**, it's valuable to have a thought process at your disposal because *winging it* can cause you to miss such factors and, therefore, prioritize poorly.

Bullshit alert: If you perform an online search, you'll find hundreds of prioritization systems out there. Some of them are incredibly complicated, with more extreme examples suggesting you label tasks by urgency and importance, rank them numerically, sort them by the estimated time necessary for completion, and use this to form a **Priority** matrix. While I appreciate the intention, such approaches are unnecessarily convoluted, even for prioritizing complex goals. Don't fall into the trap of organizational fetishism. You'll spend more time organizing your tasks than you will executing on them, and this can foster a false sense of accomplishment.

Here's a simple and effective thought process: If something new requires your attention and you need to fit it within a **Hot List** or **Goal Scaffold** of related tasks—and there are no dependencies involved—place it at the very top, compare it to the task below it, and:

1. Ask the question, "Which, if any, has a more pressing deadline?" Maybe Samantha is competing in a knife-throwing competition next Thursday, while Garrett simply wants to refresh all of his high-end kitchenware.
2. Ask the question, "Which, if any, could cause potential problems if put off?" To use an example you might find on a *General personal* **Hot List**, you probably want to fix a broken window before it rains in lieu of shopping for a new bowling ball.

3. Ask the question, "Which, if any, involves financial considerations? What are they?" If you don't pay the bathroom floor contractor on time, you may incur a late fee. If you need to decide between that and buying a fancy new coffee maker, the priority becomes obvious.

4. If it makes sense at the top, leave it. If you had to perform a swap, repeat the same comparison along with the next peer task, over and over until the new one lands in an appropriate place. Once it has, review the entire group of tasks to ensure the overall order still makes sense after introducing the latest item.

Hot List Maintenance

Hot Lists need to be curated occasionally; sometimes tasks age out after being pushed down a few times by more pressing items, so don't be afraid to dump tasks you're probably never going to get around to—tasks that provide no value and for which dumping would introduce no risk.

Consider this example: A few years ago, I was suddenly reminded of a lunch pail full of cassette tapes I always listened to as a kid, including some carefully curated mixtapes I made of all of my favorite music. Overcome with nostalgia, I resolved to find them. I was sure the lunch pail was in my basement or attic somewhere (or maybe my aunt's), and before I forgot, I placed this item in a *General personal* **Hot List**. It was low-**Priority** because, as you can imagine, it was in no way urgent—no deadline, no problems introduced by putting it off, no financial considerations, etc.

After about a year, this item was still hanging out near the bottom of the **Hot List**, constantly displaced by higher-**Priority** items. Finally, I just got rid of it. Sure, it wasn't causing any harm aside from cluttering up my list, but it's a good idea to ask yourself now and again if a lingering task is really going to provide any value, or if its presence is devaluing the rest of the items on your **Hot List**. I asked myself, "What would happen if I just deleted this?" In the big picture, the answer was, "absolutely nothing," so I dumped it and never looked back. If I really want to take a trip down memory lane while blasting a grainy cassette version of Poison's "Cry Tough," I can certainly reconsider at a later date.

Use your head, and most importantly, respect your **Hot Lists** by ensuring they're not polluted by low-class citizens—forgotten stragglers and relics of intentions and whims past. Your **Hot Lists** are not journals or reminders; they're a record of your intention to act.

Test Cases: Ensuring Completeness

When you craft an **M-SMART Goal**, you define criteria by which you could say you executed or failed to execute on your overarching intention. However, it can be easy to make assumptions and neglect specifics relating to what *complete* means when it comes to the more granular **Minor Tasks** that comprise it. In the interest of **Intentionality** and structure, there's value in building **Minor Tasks** that include information that lets you know when it's OK to move on.

For example, if you've started a woodworking/furniture business, you may find yourself facing the **Minor Task**, *Build chairs*, deep within your **Goal Scaffold**:

- Build initial demonstration furniture
  - Build a kitchen set
    - Build chairs

However, at what point could you say each chair was *built*? To solve this problem, you could include a **Test Case**—a term and concept borrowed from software engineering—in the list of **Minor Tasks** that comprise the **Major Task** you're hoping to accomplish. A **Test Case** describes a state that can only exist or an event that can only successfully take place when a task has been satisfactorily completed. For example, a simple and facetious **Test Case** for building chairs could involve *sitting down and not having your ass hit the floor*—once your **Test Case** passes, you know you've built something ass-height that could pass as a chair. More practically, you can create detailed **Test Cases** that check for more specific criteria that let you know when a **Minor Task** has been completed enough to move on.

- Build chairs
    - Sketch rough designs
    - Refine designs
    - Take measurements
    - List all wood needs
    - Collect tools and charge those that are portable
    - Purchase supplies (wood, sandpaper, stain, lacquer, screws, wood glue)
    - Cut the wood to the appropriate shapes/sizes for each chair piece
    - Sand the wood (rough)
    - Glue and screw the chairs together
    - Run structural **Test Cases**
        - Place a level on each of the chairs' surfaces; each should be level
        - Have a 150- to 250-pound adult sit in the chairs; they should each support the weight without collapsing or bowing
    - Sand the chairs (fine sanding)
    - Stain the chairs
    - Lacquer the chairs
    - Run aesthetic **Test Cases**
        - Sit on each chair and shift around for a bit; no rough areas should be noticeable
        - Hold a flashlight against all chair surfaces at a sharp angle; lacquer should appear evenly distributed, and all surfaces should seem adequately covered

Notice that the **Test Cases** are worded such that the first half describes the nature of the measurement method, while the second describes the state that should fail until you've accomplished all necessary tasks.

This is a simple extension of themes you've already explored—refining your intentions, setting high standards for your organizational **Behaviors**, and providing as much detail as possible.

WHEN?

You've now learned the *how* of managing complexity; but *when* will you put this knowledge into practice? Or, as asked in the terminology of **Personal Culture**, *what new* **Behaviors** *and* **Traditions** *can you implement to ensure you dedicate time to the things you value?*

The answer lies, of course, in **Blocked Time**. But first, let's get philosophical.

A New Definition of "Time Management"

How would you define **Time Management**?

Traditionally, **Time Management** refers to performing tasks in a certain way, in a certain order, and at certain times or within certain time frames in order to get more done in a shorter amount of time, or something of that nature. I've always loved a quote by author Charles Richards: "Don't be fooled by the calendar. There are only as many days in the year as you make use of. One man gets only a week's value out of a year while another man gets a full year's value out of a week." By this traditional definition, much of this book is about **Time Management**.

However, this is only a small part of something larger. Something deeper. Something more *human*. To understand what I mean, first consider the following: our time on this planet can be broken down into two parts— things we *have to do* and things we *want to do*.

Without getting bogged down in details about the fundamental concept of free will, we effectively *have* to do certain things under normal circumstances in order to live our lives the way we've crafted them. For most of us, this means we *have* to maintain some source of income. We *have* to remove garbage from our homes. We *have* to go to the dentist to make sure our teeth don't rot.

On the other hand, there are things we *want* to do. Under most normal circumstances, we *want* to spend time with our loved ones, we *want* to eat delicious food, and we *want* to feel emotionally fulfilled. We *want* to stay healthy and spend time doing things we enjoy.

Additionally, there are a few things that fall into both categories. For most people, sleep falls into this category. We need to sleep—we have a biological requirement for it—but aren't there times when you can't wait to go to sleep? After you're exhausted from a long day?

What things do you *have* to do? What things do you *want* to do? It's from this distinction that I propose **The Franklin Principle**.

The Franklin Principle

The Franklin Principle is the idea that *meticulously organizing the things you have to do lets you maximize uninterrupted time with which you can guiltlessly do what you want to do*. That's a superior approach to **Time Management**, as it presents a broad solution to the largest and most ubiquitous challenges you face when pursuing ambitious undertakings: you *want* to work toward your goals, but life is full of things you *have* to do.

I named **The Franklin Principle** after Ben Franklin, who was—to say the least—an interesting guy. In his roughly eighty-four years on this earth, Franklin became an accomplished inventor, founder, and the author of everything from almanacs to autobiographies. He retired comfortably at forty-two with wealth he accumulated from a printing company, furthered our understanding of electricity, participated in the creation of the Declaration of Independence and the Constitution of the United States, and served as US ambassador to France. And this is just the tip of the iceberg; in short, the man knew how to execute.

How did he get this all done?

Take a look at an example from Franklin's own account of his daily schedule from *The Autobiography of Benjamin Franklin*:

5 to 7 a.m.	*Rise, wash, and address "Powerful Goodness!" Contrive day's business and take the resolution of the day; prosecute the present study; and breakfast*
8 to 11 a.m.	*Work*
12 to 1 p.m.	*Read or overlook my accounts, and dine*
2 to 5 p.m.	*Work*
6 to 9 p.m.	*Put things in their places, supper, music, or diversion, or conversation; examination of the day*
10 p.m. to 4 a.m.	*Sleep*

With very few exceptions, Franklin knew what he would be doing during every hour of every day. He organized his time into specific sessions of **Blocked Time**, each dedicated to the furthering of a specific project or work track. He respected these sessions, and even though they were self-prescribed, he treated them as though they were defined by a ruthless supervisor. Franklin also took fun seriously (no, really—look it up), and actually blocked off time for it (6 to 9 p.m.: *music, or diversion, or conversation*). He didn't let any **Have-to-Dos** interrupt his fun, and despite being a notorious partier, he never let his **Want-to-Dos** get in the way of getting work done. His prodigious track record of execution was seemingly possible partly due to his having learned to say, *There's a time for that, but now is not that time.*

The above is admittedly a broad example (for instance, what exactly does "work" entail?), but if you dig deeply into his writings, you'll see he broke his sessions of **Blocked Time** down into much more detail. He socialized his **Behaviors** and **Traditions** to those around him, both professionally and personally. He started on time and ended on time.

He wasn't the only prodigious historical figure to adhere to a detailed, block-based schedule; other noteworthy individuals cited **Behaviors** and **Traditions** like these as vital to their success. Theodore Roosevelt was arguably just as prodigious a character as Franklin. Browsing his impressive résumé, you'd find that he was president of the United States and a Nobel Peace Prize recipient. He authored dozens of books on a wide range of subjects. His interests were broad, and he could famously talk into the wee hours on virtually any topic. How did such a unique character organize his time?

Take a look at a breakdown of a day on the campaign trail, excerpted from *The Rise of Theodore Roosevelt* by Edmund Morris:

7 a.m.	*Breakfast*	**2:30 p.m.**	*Reading Sir Walter Scott*
7:30 a.m.	*A speech*	**3 p.m.**	*Answering telegrams*
8 a.m.	*Reading a historical work*	**3:45 p.m.**	*A speech*
9 a.m.	*A speech*	**4 p.m.**	*Meeting the press*
10 a.m.	*Dictating letters*	**4:30 p.m.**	*Reading*
11 a.m.	*Discussing Montana mines*	**5 p.m.**	*A speech*

11:30 a.m.	A speech		**6 p.m.**	Reading
12 p.m.	Reading an ornithological work		**7 p.m.**	Supper
12:30 p.m.	A speech		**8 p.m.**	Speaking
1 p.m.	Lunch		**11 p.m.**	Reading alone in car
1:30 p.m.	A speech		**12 p.m.**	To bed

As you can see, Roosevelt's time was broken into small blocks. This isn't surprising, given the fact that time spent on the campaign trail implies time-sensitive obligations; however, consider that at noon, Roosevelt was reading about birds. This obviously had nothing to do with his campaign or his political career, but was rather something he *wanted* to do. How could Roosevelt justify this without feeling pressured or rushed? How did one of the most powerful men in the world—arguably one of the *busiest* men in the world—have time to read about birds while campaigning to retain the presidency of the United States?

Or history (8 a.m.)? Or the works of Sir Walter Scott (2:30 p.m.)?

If Roosevelt had just tried to fit leisure reading in *when he had time*, do you think he'd have been able to do it? What you're seeing Roosevelt do in the above schedule is *true* **Time Management**: using meticulous organization to take and protect time for the things that mattered to him.

To quote author Kerry Johnson, "Do we need more time? Or do we need to be more disciplined with the time we have?"

The Franklin Principle in Your Own Life

Remember our new definition of **Time Management**: to meticulously organize the things you *have to do* in order to maximize uninterrupted time with which you can guiltlessly do what you *want to do*.

Uninterrupted. Guiltlessly. These are important words.

Imagine the following example: You wake up on Saturday morning and want to relax. You had a rough week, and before beginning any chores, you want to kick back for an hour or so and watch some mindless television. However, you know the lawn needs to be mowed (or a window frame needs to be caulked, or the bathroom needs to be cleaned, or cupcakes need to be baked for a school event), and it's your responsibility. While trying to relax, you're invariably going to suffer from some degree of pressure about the impending chore. It may be subtle—a mere shadow in the deepest recesses of your mind—or it may be blatant—haunting your every thought. Either way, the whole time, you know deep down that you really *should* be getting to that chore.

Feel familiar?

On top of this, internal sources of pressure are met with external sources, as spouses, family members, roommates, and parents all contribute to this weight. Of course, you can say, "I'll mow the lawn after I watch these cartoons," and everyone around you can acknowledge your promise and seem to accept it, but is it really that simple? Is the guilt and pressure really gone? Can you truly enjoy your **Want-to-Do**, or has the **Have-to-Do** infiltrated the experience? At any given time, you most likely have dozens of responsibilities you need to get around to; while they wait in line, will you truly enjoy what you're doing or be able to fully engage?

Let's further explore the psychology behind this. Assume your job functions on a typical office schedule (Monday to Friday, 9 a.m. to 5 p.m.). If that's the case, barring any extraordinary circumstances, it's unlikely that you'd suddenly find yourself on the couch on Saturday morning saying, "I really feel like I should be at work."

Why not?

The reason is simple: You've established set, defined times you're *supposed* to be at work, and because of this distinction, you allow yourself to step away from it—guilt-free—when it's appropriate to do so. This is part of the **Culture** surrounding your relationship with work (**Behaviors, Traditions**). Anyone affected by your being at work or not being at work understands why you aren't there on Saturday morning. This makes perfect sense for your job, but with many of the **Have-to-Dos** in your personal life (such as the chores mentioned), you don't make these same distinctions; rather, you let them pile up in a shapeless, guilt-inducing backlog, from which you're expected to pluck the next chore whenever the opportunity presents itself.

This is not conducive to properly separating life's **Have-to-Dos** and **Want-to-Dos**, as your **Have-to-Dos** will constantly haunt you while engaging in your **Want-to-Dos**. We're completely used to this feeling, and as such, this anxiety and pressure is an accepted part of modern life—a grim, subtle weight bearing down on us from above, compounding and causing everything from vague irritation to measurable hypertension.

You're being robbed of your right to the *present* by your **Have-to-Dos**. It doesn't have to be this way.

The solution is simple: If you define a specific time and duration for a specific chore (or type of chore), you'll be less prone to feel the task looming over you. This is because until the time arrives, it *simply isn't the appropriate time*, just as it isn't time for work yet on Saturday morning. If you subscribe to this way of doing things, socialize it, and exhibit **Behaviors** that demonstrate that you take it seriously, you'll alter your **Personal Culture**, slowly build trust among those around you, and find that you'll shed feelings of pressure about **Have-to-Dos**—feelings you may not even be aware you're currently harboring. Commit to mowing the lawn at 11:30 a.m. sharp, and don't let yourself begin even a minute late. Treat the **Blocked Time** with respect, and you'll slowly train those around you to respect it, as well. That's **The Franklin Principle**. That's *real* **Time Management**.

Counterintuitively, this type of meticulous organization will simplify your life whether you have two or two thousand responsibilities. I think we can all relate to the experience of focusing on mental to-do lists when we should be engaging with loved ones or enjoying ourselves. If you find yourself struggling with anxiety you can trace back to an inability to mentally detach from your responsibilities, I encourage you to shoo away the thoughts with the mantra, *There's a time for that, but now is not that time.*

By organizing the things he had to do—by blocking off specific time for both work and play—Roosevelt let himself have his bird-reading fun without needing to feel any guilt or anxiety about it. He created separation, and you don't need presidential authority to do the same; you simply need patience as those around you adjust to your new approach and the trust it requires.

The Art of Taking

In order to block off time for **Want-to-Dos** (like your goals), you have to first understand and accept that you can't just *fit things in*. That model rarely works for anyone, and if you're honest with yourself, I think you'll agree it's failed you, as well. If you want to get something done—if it's truly valuable or important to you—then you need to grant it the dedicated time it deserves. You can't *find* time, and you can't *make* time, but you can *take* time.

Say those three statements aloud and really think about each, as well as the distinctions between them: You can't *find* time. You can't *make* time. But you can *take* time.

These three sentences demonstrate a shift in **Language**—both internally and in communicating with others—that conveys that time is something you have considerable (albeit specific) control over. You can't *find* or *make* time because time is, by definition, a finite resource. When you're born, you've been granted an inheritance. Most of us have been handed a huge amount of wealth in the only truly global currency: time. This is why people talk about how they *spend* their time. Everything you do costs you a bit of this currency, and—while you can live healthfully and try to elongate the tail end of your life—you can't truly *make* time. There are twenty-four hours in the days of the both the laziest and the most productive individuals on Earth. However, you can *take* time; you can tactically deprioritize or displace other responsibilities—responsibilities with inflated priority due to recency bias, short-term vision, perceived urgency, routine, or others' wishes.

This shift in **Language** should empower you. Shift your **Personal Culture's Values** and decide that you'll no longer tolerate passivity in your relationship with time. Resolve to stop speaking in lamentations and commiseration, despite how embedded they are in the **Language** of Western culture. We all have excuses—we're all tired, we're all busy—but you can decide what matters to you. That TV show? Drinks with friends after work? An unnecessary extra half-hour of sleep? Playing dumb games on your phone while you're on the bus to work? Or making progress toward your goals? Your side business? Your novel? Your art? Your relationship with your child? Your career growth or career change? Your studies?

Accept that you have considerable control over the finite time you have, and that—under normal circumstances—your decisions to engage in all but the most necessary acts are indeed decisions.

There isn't a single person with whom I've shared this **Behavior** who hasn't been able to take a little time each week for something they value. That's not an exaggeration. No matter how much responsibility they had, everyone I've worked with has been able to take useful chunks of time back from the rhythms of their lives—this includes executives, business owners, entertainers, attorneys, and even a mother of young twins. I know how difficult it can be to adopt these **Behaviors**; we each think we're an exception, and that our days and lives are somehow busier than everyone else's. That our jobs are stricter. That we can't build the appropriate trust and that we're not in a position to influence the **Culture** that surrounds us.

Remind yourself about this approach from time to time when working toward goals, and start using your new **Language** in response to others' requests for your time: "Yeah, I can *take* the time to do that." Once you begin using this terminology, you'll begin to think about **Time Management** in an intention-driven manner. It will force you to face and convey to others the fact that you're either willing or unwilling to spend currency (time) on *x* instead of *y*—currency you'll never get back.

I'm certainly no Franklin or Roosevelt, but I can personally attest to the power of **The Franklin Principle**. In many ways, it's responsible for my remaining effective and low-stress while simultaneously writing thousands of pages of content for books, articles, and programs, serving as a senior technology leader in demanding corporate environments, tackling ambitious personal and creative projects, speaking at events, and pursuing new skills. It's responsible for this very book—not in some abstract way, but directly: I used these **Behaviors** to bring this book to life while juggling a vast number of other responsibilities and still managing to be an attentive husband, father, son, and friend. It's kept me perfectly sane when my life probably looked unsustainable to an outsider. Had I simply "fit writing in when I had the time," you wouldn't be reading this right now because I can tell you without question that this book never would have never come to be. Only by sectioning off non-negotiable sessions of **Blocked Time** was I able to dedicate enough time and energy to progress at a reasonable rate. I didn't *find* the time. I didn't *make* the time. I *took* the time. I've done the same thing for fitness goals, personal goals, creative goals—the list goes on and on. Every valuable **Want-to-Do** is given the proper time and organization, and every **Have-to-Do** is isolated, communicated, and executed on. Perhaps most importantly, I promise you I'm not up at night worrying about what I may have forgotten or missed.

And if I *can't* take the time to address a desire or project, it forces me to ask the sometimes-difficult question of whether or not it's truly valuable or important to me. Something may seem important in the moment, and this process forces you to truly assess its value. This is a healthy and natural filtration system for those who—like me—are easily enthused.

It's deceivingly simple, but I promise you it works:

Take the **Blocked Time**. Arrive at the **Blocked Time**. Use your **Script**. Use your **Hot List**.

Take the **Blocked Time**. Arrive at the **Blocked Time**. Use your **Script**. Use your **Hot List**.

Most people would agree that there are multiple factors that contribute to success, whatever their definition of success may be. However, I argue that this **Behavior** is the one most universally shared across some of the greatest success stories in history, as well as in the lives and careers of the greatest leaders I've worked for and the most interesting people I've ever met. I'll take it a step further and say that I believe this **Behavior** is the one most universally ignored by those who are constantly making excuses and trying to catch up.

Blocked Time

We've obviously touched on **Blocked Time**, but let's look at it in more detail.

Living The Franklin Principle

Let's go through an example that marries both professional and personal sessions of **Blocked Time** into one calendar. In this fictional scenario, this individual—let's call her "Janet"—works for a print/digital magazine. We'll explore how she uses **Scripts** and **Hot Lists** to make use of the time she dedicates to both her **Have-to-Dos** and **Want-to-Dos**.

Time	Activity	Time	Activity
9 a.m.	**BLOCKED TIME:** *Work*	**2 p.m.**	*Weekly marketing team meeting*
10 a.m.	*Meeting with Joan C.*	**3 p.m.**	*Interview new journalist prospect*
10:30 a.m.	*Review committee proposal*	**4 p.m.**	*Daily wrap-up meeting*
12 p.m.	**BLOCKED TIME:** *Work*	**5:30 p.m.**	**BLOCKED TIME:** *Study German*
12:30 p.m.	*Lunch*	**8:30 p.m.**	**BLOCKED TIME:** *Irish dance*
1 p.m.	*Meeting with Sean S.*	**10 p.m.**	*Bed*

Janet sections off two sessions of **Blocked Time** during her workday. In the first, you could imagine that she comes into the office, gets settled, and goes through a *Work* **Daily Script** not unlike the one we used as an earlier example—she responds to emails, makes notes for the day's meetings, etc.:

1. Check work email and voicemail and reply as needed
2. Assess any new items you need to keep track of and add them to your **Hot List**
3. Check your calendar; review the day's meetings and prepare notes for each
4. Perform daily repeated tasks
5. Address your *Work* **Hot List**

Then she spends the rest of the hour working on her *Work* **Hot List** once directed there from her **Script**. She ignores her emails and phone during the **Blocked Time**, and if someone pops into her workspace and makes a request, she either asks them to come back later or quickly jots a note about it on her *Work* **Hot List**. At 10 a.m. sharp, she stops because she has other responsibilities; even if she's in the middle of a task, she doesn't let herself go over by even a few seconds. At 12 p.m., she begins another session of **Blocked Time** and again focuses on *Work* **Hot List** tasks until she eats lunch and relaxes at 12:30 p.m.

From what you've learned so far in this book, you should recognize the benefits of approaching the day in this structured way. Among them:

- Isolating sessions of **Blocked Time** and focusing on only the current **Script/Hot List** item (as well as enforcing a *not-now* **Culture** for anyone trying to infiltrate) lets Janet focus and either defer incoming tasks or quickly place them in her *Work* **Hot List** to be properly prioritized.
- Using a **Script** and a **Hot List** to keep her on task reduces context switching and the efficiency lost in context switching (we'll explore this further shortly).
- Using a **Script** and a **Hot List** helps her manage anxiety since nothing will get lost or require her to use her memory alone to track tasks or responsibilities.
- These organizational **Behaviors** will build trust and the impression of responsibility over time as her ability to keep track of and address multiple ongoing bodies of work improves.

Please note: This example highlights how **Blocked Time** can help manage complexity for those who have jobs for whom schedules are fluid, but responsibilities tend to collect—such as is the case with managers, knowledge workers, administrative assistants, project managers, realtors, finance professionals, and salespeople. If Janet had a different type of job entirely—one with fundamental consistency (data entry or factory work) or one hinged on customer interaction (retail or food service), for instance—she may find it much more difficult to block off time during her workday, and doing so may not provide as much value.

The next section of the example is applicable to anyone, however. On the personal side of things, imagine that Janet is trying to learn German, since a close family friend moved to Berlin, and she promised to visit him one day. Learning a new language is notoriously difficult for adults, so this is a great example of an endeavor that requires regular practice and would get nowhere if she was simply "fitting it in when she can." When she's on the train home at the end of the day, instead of playing games on her phone, chatting with friends, or reading, she studies German. She's well aware she could spend that time engaged in a leisure activity, but learning German is a **Want-to-Do** she values enough to ensure she's giving it the structure it needs.

When she steps on the train and gets settled, her calendar beeps and reminds her it's time for a German session. First, she takes a look at her *German* **Script**:

- Review verb list
- Review the list of phrases I'm having difficulty with
- Consult *German* **Hot List**

Once she goes through her **Script's** first two steps, she finds herself directed to her *German* **Hot List** (which, since it lays out the end-to-end instructions for her goal, we can call a **Goal Scaffold**). She references it to determine where she left off (in this case, we could imagine that it points her to Chapter 6 of an audio course she's working through) and continues from there.

Later that night, while her husband gives their kids a bath, she goes into the garage and works on learning Irish dance, another **Want-to-Do** she's been interested in since childhood but never had the time to pursue. She now blocks off a little time every Thursday night and Sunday morning for it. Much like German- and job-centric sessions of **Blocked Time**, she starts promptly, ends promptly, and consults her **Script** and eventually her **Hot List** for Irish dance. She even uses a timer to let herself know when she only has five minutes left.

She socializes it; she tells her husband and kids about the **Blocked Time**. Her parents and friends know not to call (and even if they do, her phone will be in a different room). Janet knows that this can be a big shift in mentality for those around her, so she lets people know *why* blocking off this time was important to her. With time and rigidity, she builds a **Culture** of trust within her family; they know she'll be available again at 9 p.m. sharp and can therefore work around the **Blocked Time**. In doing so, she can focus on these goals without guilt, pressure, or anxiety. She also lets her family know that, in return for their leaving her alone, she'll be respectful of their **Blocked Time** if they choose to pursue their own **Want-to-Dos**.

Janet's schedule may seem obnoxiously strict, but without building this structure and adhering to it, she's probably going to fail at learning German and Irish dance. She faces the same choice you'll have to face whenever you consider a goal's value: you can live a completely flexible, fly-by-the-seat-of-your-pants life, or you can embrace serious organization, properly manage complexity, and accomplish the things you want to accomplish. You can't have both.

Executor Insight

"For me, to get anything done, I have to do it every day for a minimum amount of time. It is remarkable how good you can get if you do something every day for thirty minutes over a period of several years. For example, I read for thirty minutes a day…no exceptions. No excuses. Flu, traveling, broke up with girlfriend, whatever. I have to read thirty minutes. People talk about

> *'deliberate practice' and that it's important how you spend your
> time practicing. But for me, that's the easy part. The hard part,
> and the one that most people fail at, is to stick with it, day after
> day, without quitting when it gets tough. I am constantly
> surprised at how many excuses my brain can generate to avoid
> doing a thirty-minute activity. That's why it's not easy. When you
> don't feel like doing it, stop thinking, and just do it."*
>
> —Lex Fridman
> Machine Learning Research Scientist at MIT | Interviewed in 2015

Let's discuss some best practices in detail.

You May Be Many Yous

Notice that in the above example, Janet didn't create **Blocked Time** for *Personal Interests*, but rather specifically for German and Irish dance. While some goals may be simple and warrant generic **Blocked Time**, defining specific sessions may be vital in other cases.

I once spoke with an agent/manager who represented extreme athletes, and while he employed an assistant, he was stressed out to a degree I couldn't exaggerate if I tried. He was already blocking off parts of his day for work, family, self-care, etc.—a rare-but-crucial practice for the self-employed—but when he faced work time, he found himself addressing tasks that fell into a wide range of themes. During the brief time I was speaking with him, he received questions about payments via email, took a call about work visas for a Canadian BMX athlete entering Singapore, and handled something else work-related via text (he didn't share details, but he shook his head, rubbed his eyes, and sighed audibly).

As I explained to him, while he existed in a single body, he was functionally performing the jobs of over a dozen separate individuals: a

77

business owner, a project manager, an artist relations professional, an accountant, an IT consultant, a sponsorship coordinator, a branding and marketing manager, a mentor (and occasional therapist), a career coach, an operations professional, and a travel agent, among others. Instead of dedicating sessions of **Blocked Time** to *work* (generically), I asked him to dedicate specific sessions and resources to each individual work track on which he needed to focus—to create **Scripts**, **Hot Lists**, and **Blocked Time** for the business owner version of himself, other **Scripts**, **Hot Lists**, and **Blocked Time** for the sponsorship coordinator, and so on. In doing so—and in being diligent about ensuring that each resource and session of **Blocked Time** remained untouched by the other work tracks or versions of himself—he could work efficiently, reduce stress, and improve his rate of progress. Perhaps most importantly, each work track's priorities would remain independent and would never need to compete. For instance, instead of having to compare the urgency of *securing a website domain name for a motocross athlete's upcoming memoir* against *determining which hotels are closest to an arena in Arizona*, the former could exist at the top of the IT consultant's **Hot List** and the latter at the top of the travel agent's **Hot List**—to be addressed during each work track's respective **Blocked Time**. Never the two tasks shall meet.

Starting on Time and Ending on Time

When you dedicate a session of **Blocked Time** to a **Want-to-Do** or **Have-to-Do**, *start on time*, and just as importantly, *end on time*.

Starting on time makes perfect sense—doing so is a fundamental function of discipline ingrained in us since childhood—but many people overlook the importance of *ending on time*.

Even if you're on a roll and everything is going really well, stop your sessions of **Blocked Time** when your allotted time is up—not a second later. Over time, this will train you to work efficiently. *Parkinson's Law* states that the amount of time *required* to perform a task is directly related to the amount of time *allotted* to perform the task; that's why it took you two weeks to write a report in school when it was due in two weeks but only took you two hours when it was due the next day. If you acknowledge that sessions of **Blocked Time**—like all time, in the larger sense—are finite, then when you realize time is running out for a specific session, you'll focus on what's important and work effectively.

Treating Blocked Time with Respect

Once you have sessions of **Blocked Time** allocated and have committed to starting and ending on time, you need to treat the time with respect.

Let's illustrate this with an example to which most people can relate. Imagine that your boss blocked off a half-hour to meet with you, and then a peer tried to book you for that same time slot. You'd feel justified in saying, "I can't meet then. I have something," because you see your meeting with the boss as something you really shouldn't move. You respect it.

This makes sense—your boss is your boss. However, this proves that you can defer or reasonably refuse others' requests for your time without the world ending. If you block off your *own* personal or professional time, you likely treat it with much less respect. Your own time is always the first to be compromised when you encounter a conflict; it's human nature. Unfortunately, your **Want-to-Dos** and **Have-to-Dos** need **Blocked Time**, so you have to shift your mentality.

While **Blocked Time** can be used in both your private and professional endeavors, it's especially important to build a **Culture** of respect around it during private time, as this is when you're most likely to work on tasks that relate to personal goals. There's an art to saying, "I can't do that at that time," when reasonable, without the conversation being uncomfortable. In many cases, the right delivery can ease any impressions of rudeness or disrespect, especially if you share context/justification and proactively work with the requester to find a different time that works for you both. Consider the long-term gain that could come with making progress toward your goal and weigh that against the perceived urgency of any task or time being asked of you by others. Weigh that gain against your anxieties about the impression you think you're creating by saying no. We often default to saying "yes" instead of truly considering the value of what's being requested and deciding whether it's something worth spending **Time Currency** on. Ask yourself what Ben Franklin would do. If you're still having trouble creating and defending **Blocked Time** after communicating your goals and justifications to those who may try to claim your time, you may have larger issues to address in the **Cultures** that surround you.

Blocking your own time at your job—as our fictional friend Janet did—can seem even more uncomfortable, but this is one of the first things I ask of emerging or developing leaders I work with. If one of my employees ever came to me and said, "Listen, I've been having a hard time getting things done and leaving at a reasonable time with all of these meetings—I want to block off my first hour of each day to catch up, prepare, and work on valuable projects," I would absolutely encourage them to do so. In fact, I would challenge them to take even *more* time, and if their proposed "first hour" timing posed problems for any reason, I would collaborate with them to identify times that work better. That's how important I believe **Blocked Time** is. If socialized properly and used to its fullest by responsible individuals, professional **Blocked Time** almost always adds value.

Treating **Blocked Time** with respect goes beyond interactions—it also requires changing some specific **Behaviors**. When it's time to focus on a goal or undertaking (or, as phrased in the **Language** of this book, when it's time to engage in **Blocked Time**), you need to be effective and productive. Effectiveness and productivity have several natural enemies, the most ubiquitous and damaging being *lack of motivation, interruption*, and *inability to focus*. When you're unmotivated or unable to focus, it's difficult to work effectively; and when you're interrupted, you're *prevented* from working effectively, despite any intentions or motivation. You waste your **Time Currency**. To avoid these enemies, you can take simple steps to reduce your likelihood of engaging in effectiveness- and productivity-eroding **Behaviors**. I call such **Behaviors** *junk food* because—like cookies, candy, and potato chips—they seem to be available nearly everywhere, and while they may feel good in the moment, they're detrimental in the longer term.

These simple steps aren't novel, by any means, and they have been advocated *ad nauseam* not just by productivity gurus, parents, and teachers, but also your inner conscience. You *know* they work.

So why am I bothering to include them? First, if I omitted them, I suppose I'd be doing a disservice to the few who sincerely may have never considered them or their value. For everyone else, I know as well as anyone that a reminder will sometimes help kickstart good **Behaviors**.

Junk Food #1: Relying on Motivation

Note that we're talking about *motivation* (singular), not *motivations* (plural). *Motivations* (plural) were addressed when we discussed **CMV** and **M-SMART Goals**. These are good.

Motivation (singular), on the other hand, refers to *short-term enthusiasm* or *immediate drive*.

If you're unmotivated, it can be difficult to work effectively. However, this is only true if you give motivation or lack of motivation the power to influence your effectiveness, and you should never do so. While motivation will rarely hurt you, it's fleeting, fickle, and impractical for reasons you'll understand shortly. When it comes to goals you value, you need to instead set up a framework that forces you to execute uniformly regardless of the presence of motivation—a framework that strips lack of motivation of its power entirely. You'll become familiar with such a framework soon, when you explore the third **Foundation of Execution**.

Until you learn that, I encourage you to grow skeptical and dismissive of any **Culture** of superficial motivation that you encounter in the wild.

Roll your eyes every time your social media feed wastes your precious attention and **Time Currency** with an inspirational quote set over a stock photo of a mountain. Every time a content marketer reminds you that *you're a warrior* and drowns you in hashtags about *crushing your day*. Every time a wellness guru tells you that in simply living joyously, your goals are all but met.

Junk Food #2: Setting Yourself up to Fall Victim to Interruption

When you're working on something you value, I'm willing to bet you either expose yourself to interruption even though you know better, or you *think* you're protecting yourself from it but are actually doing a terrible job of doing so. Either way, you need to take interruption seriously, because it may be more damaging to your effectiveness and productivity than you think.

Imagine that you're working on something when an email comes in. Since it will only take a moment, you decide to check it. Either it *wasn't* important, and you've just wasted a minute—or it *was* important, and now you're distracted. Familiar, right? When you're interrupted from a task that requires focus, it takes a certain amount of time to fully recover from the distraction. This recovery time is the most obvious (and most easily quantifiable) cost of interruption, and it chips away at effectiveness and productivity in measurable ways. While recovery time varies from person to person, some experts suggest that it takes more than *twenty-three minutes* to fully restore your focus to the level it was at before the distraction occurred.

To demonstrate the time cost of interruption, imagine that you take only one minute (an extremely conservative number according to most research) to recover from a significant, context-switching interruption and reengage with your original task. Using this one-minute number, imagine that you've been working on a project for an hour, and you were interrupted *once* for *five minutes*; this means you were only working for fifty-four minutes, because you were interrupted for five minutes plus one minute of context-switching recovery time.

$$60m - (1 \times 5m) - (1 \times 1m) = 54m$$

However, if you were interrupted *five times* for *one minute each*—as is more common with emails, texts, or in-person questions—you now have *five* individual one-minute refocus periods to overcome, which amounts to *five minutes* of wasted time. The total interruption time is the same (5 minutes), but you've lost a good deal of time realigning your focus.

$$60m - (5 \times 1m) - (5 \times 1m) = 50m$$

This may not seem like much, but if you're only working on goals, projects, and tasks for half-hour or hour-long sessions of **Blocked Time**, interruptions can add up. You're most likely so accustomed to constant distractions that you don't even realize how common they are.

There are other costs to interruption that can be harder to quantify. Research shows that even when people seem to recover well from interruptions (as measured by the amount of time needed to complete similar tasks while focused vs. while interrupted), the interruptions still measurably increase stress and frustration[1].

---

[1] If you're interested in diving more deeply into this topic, I suggest you look up *The Cost of Interrupted Work: More Speed and Stress* by Gloria Mark (UC Irvine) and Daniela Gudith & Ulrich Klocke (Humboldt University).

Lastly, there's creativity cost, perhaps the most critical (and least-quantifiable) type of damage caused by interruption. In being interrupted, you could very well lose track of your train of thought and forever forfeit a valuable, creative idea.

Interruption can be broken into two threats: **Outgoing Interruption** and **Incoming Interruption**.

Outgoing Interruption refers to self-induced interruption—browsing your phone unprompted, sending emails, engaging with social media, texting friends, seeking out in-person conversations, and daydreaming. Devices are perhaps the biggest culprits; we're so used to the sense of community and connectivity associated with our devices that their presence is engrained into our central nervous system in non-trivial and fascinating ways. Individuals will often find themselves reaching for their mobile devices without even realizing they're doing so or feeling naked without having them on their person.

Navigating around and resisting the allures of this type of interruption can be difficult, and many individuals try to do so through simple self-discipline. However, self-discipline—like motivation—is unreliable, at best. As a society, we're enamored by the wisdom and advice of the those who overtly display self-discipline **Behaviors**, and we assume we can implement them ourselves. If this were true, proper nutrition, studying, exercise, and reasonable bedtimes would probably be much more commonplace.

The best way to reduce **Outgoing Interruption** is by altering your physical surroundings when engaging in **Blocked Time**. Try to isolate yourself in a room or area with minimal distractions. Remove devices and printed text from your immediate reach. Turn all televisions and music off. If you're working on a computer, mobile phone, or tablet and don't need Internet access, switch it off. If you require Internet connectivity, disable messaging and notifications; this is easy to do on almost all modern devices. Such pre-work steps should be added to any appropriate **Scripts**. Additionally, there are tools that are specifically designed to help you remain focused when at your computer by blocking access to distracting websites and services for set periods of time. New apps and services like this hit the market all the time; spend a few minutes looking into them and weighing their features against your needs. When, where, and how do you tend to lose focus? What thoughts tend to distract or interrupt you the most? Of what **Outgoing Interruption Behaviors** are you most guilty?

The other type of interruption is **Incoming**—incoming calls, texts, messages, direct human interaction, and other stimulation. Aside from minimizing your digital connectivity as mentioned, the best thing you can do to avoid this is to ensure people know not to interrupt you during **Blocked Time** unless there's an emergency. You have responsibilities— places to be, people to see, and others who rely on you for an array of needs as a caretaker, driver, and so on; an hour without you can seem much longer than it really is. While you can alter the **Culture** that surrounds you, as mentioned, doing so takes time. In addition, life can be unpredictable, and problems often arise without warning, and it can take a while to evolve beyond a mentality in which you reactively assign unearned urgency to those unexpected situations. We already covered this; how can you proactively ensure a **Culture** of respect for the time you've allocated? Update shared calendars, set away statuses in messaging apps, spread the word, and lock the door to the room.

In short, use your head. You know when your **Behaviors** are and aren't setting you up for interruption. Don't give yourself easy access to this snack.

Junk Food #3: Setting Yourself up to Lose Focus

We're operating with deeply damaged attention spans; unless you were raised by wolves or off-the-grid preppers, you've likely spent your life immersed in a culture of rapid-fire stimulation. You've spent decades dealing with parallel sources of information tugging at your neural networks like a crowd of crazed paparazzi, vying for your attention. While you can alter your **Personal Culture** and slowly develop the ability to focus for longer periods, this too can take time. Until then, an hour dedicated to a single task without distraction or connection can, at times, seem like a lifetime within the confines of your buzzing skull. If internal factors make it difficult to engage completely during sessions of **Blocked Time**, you may want to consider that the expectations you've set for your attention span may be overambitious. Resolve to take breaks or check in at specific, pre-defined intervals; doing so is less damaging to productivity than powering through in defiance of your nature or taking unstructured breaks whenever your attention span bottoms out. In scheduling breaks or check-ins:

- You'll minimize your distraction recovery time by reducing the number of individual interruptions you deal with.
- You'll more easily resist the temptation to engage in **Outgoing Interruption Behaviors** because you'll operate with the knowledge that you have an impending outlet (and, therefore, simply need to exercise patience).
- You'll likely find it easier to build a **Culture** in which others respect your time by letting them know they'll have opportunities to reach you if the need should arise.
- You'll reduce the likelihood of burnout.

For instance, set a rule that forces you to take a break for five minutes at the end of every half-hour session of **Blocked Time**. Treat the breaks with respect just as you've learned to treat your actual working time with respect: share these breaks with anyone your **Blocked Time** may affect, set and adhere to strict start and end times, leave your physical workspace for a change of scenery, and try not to think about what you're working on during your break.

Attention spans vary wildly, and some people become antsy and ineffective much more quickly than others. While working on a challenging task, you may benefit from taking a short break every twenty minutes, while that frequency may feel more like an undue interruption for someone with a higher threshold. While factors such as caffeine, executive function disorders, and interest in the task at hand could shorten or lengthen your natural **Focus Rhythms**, you can most likely loosely estimate ideal *work* and *break* durations and use them to build a template for your sessions of **Blocked Time** that maximizes effectiveness. Over time, you should be able to lengthen your working periods without lengthening your breaks.

Executor Insight

"I walk around my neighborhood several times throughout the day, and it clears the tunnel vision that occurs when I work on something for too long...taking more breaks, more often, helps me refocus and makes me more productive in total."

—Roman Bejnar
Designer/Brand Strategist | Interviewed in 2014

Determine your current **Focus Rhythms** by listening to your instincts as you implement more and more **Blocked Time**. When you're burned out and having trouble learning or producing anything more in a particular session, you know it; your brain provides clues. How long can you focus on a mentally taxing task before becoming tired, cross-eyed, or easily distracted? As long as it's over twenty minutes (for practicality purposes), set this as your default working time (round up to the nearest five-minute mark), and then set your break time to three minutes (or five if your working time is more than an hour straight). Start there. If you're unable to determine your ideal **Focus Rhythm**, start out with thirty minutes working and three minutes of break time.

Once you've settled on a template for **Blocked Time**, make no exceptions. Make it a **Tradition** and reflect the template in your **Scripts**. This is a war you're fighting: you're a human being, so you're programmed for association and, therefore, distraction. If you allow for concessions, they will only give way to further concessions and eventually lead to a breakdown of the entire system.

These types of cookies, candy, and chips have no place in your healthy **Personal Culture**. Once you've made a plan—not just a resolution—to circumvent them, continue reading.

WHAT?

A few years ago, over dinner, a friend told me about a problem he was having: Aspects of his personal life were spinning out of control. First, he missed a few appointments—a dentist's visit, a family event, and so on—but over time, he found himself losing track of more and more. He began to wake in the middle of the night with the sinking feeling he was forgetting things.

As we dug into his issue, the cause became obvious: as it turned out, my friend—a husband, father of four, manager at a major insurance company, and youth sports coach in his late thirties—had no personal calendar. None. Not on his desk, not on his wall, not in his phone. He simply tried to remember an extraordinary volume of personal and professional responsibilities in his head, and, as an unsurprising result, began losing track of things.

And it didn't end with events. He had no to-do list, sticky notes, notebook, or scribbles on the back of his hand. No collection of crumpled napkins with scrawled reminders stuffed into the pockets of his jeans.

I sat there, slack-jawed, as I came to comprehend the depth of his stress. His kids' social security numbers weren't written down. His blood type wasn't written down. The date of his last oil change, his bank account numbers, and bands his friends suggested he might enjoy were all just swirling around in his head, devoid of hierarchy or priority. He had no calendar reminder letting him know he needed to be in work early for mandatory training the following Thursday, or that his wedding anniversary was approaching, or that he had to take his Irish Wolfhound for her annual checkup.

It's not the year 1410, and—without even considering goals—you most likely have more to keep track of than you can reasonably expect to keep in your head. I gave my friend (who was admittedly an extreme case) the advice I've already shared in the pages of this book: act as though you're a project manager hired to keep track of the affairs of a small business—and imagine that small business is your life. Treat that job as though your performance was being tracked and measured. Strive to do a great job. Once you get used to this shift in mentality, its value will become evident, and the **Behaviors** you're learning will naturally carry over from your personal life into whatever ambitious projects or goals you take on.

This means your **Scripts**, **Hot Lists**, and **Blocked Time** need to exist somewhere outside your skull. There's a clinical precedent for this advice: doctors will often suggest that adults suffering from ADHD adopt the use of tools to manage their lives. While the complexities of everyday life may be enough to overwhelm someone suffering from ADHD, there's no reason the rest of us can't take advantage of the same constructs; and in a hyperconnected world, we all suffer from some degree of attention deficit brought on by external forces. Especially if you plan to launch into an ambitious undertaking—as I suspect you are, given the fact that you're holding this book in your hands—the use of tools will be vital not only to your success, but also your sanity.

The Three Execution Tools

In order to implement the strategies we've discussed, you're going to need three **Execution Tools**:

- A **Note-Taking Tool**
- A **Listing Tool**
- A **Calendar**

You're going to learn about each tool and discover how they collectively create a perfect ecosystem that represents the mental organizational model you've come to know and love. When we're done here, you'll live and die by these three tools, and they'll become core to your **Personal Culture**.

A Note-Taking Tool

There's no twist here: a **Note-Taking Tool** is a utility you use to capture, store, and reference notes. I define *notes* as detailed, medium-to-large bodies of information, which are typically comprised of sentences and paragraphs.

If I go to a class, seminar, conference, or talk, I'm likely taking a few pages of notes. I collect notes for books and presentations I'm writing or projects and programs I'm developing. Earlier, when you learned about the **Exploratory Phase**, it was mentioned that you should collect notes; this is where such notes should be captured.

Your notes should be quickly available, easily searchable, and accessible from a number of devices. Given these criteria, I wholeheartedly endorse Evernote (EVERNOTE.COM). This suggestion is the result of a good deal of trial and error on my part and the parts of individuals with whom I've shared these **Behaviors**. Evernote is a robust tool that lets you make notes out of anything; you can use your voice, clips from websites, emails, photographs, and more. However, I argue that its real power is plain text; I essentially treat Evernote like a series of digital marble notebooks.

I should probably point out that I'm not endorsed in any way by the tools I suggest in this book—they're simply the ones that seem to work best at the time of this writing.

Evernote is accessible through a desktop app, mobile apps, and web browsers. It's cloud-based, which means information is stored remotely and securely, and syncs between multiple devices; if you create, edit, or delete a note, the changes will propagate across all the devices you're using. Furthermore, you can sort notes into notebooks and add tags to notes for easy searching, which lets you intuitively organize and quickly locate notes relating to individual undertakings—something useful given your new mental organizational model.

If you don't already have an account, sign up for Evernote Basic now. As of the time of this writing, you can use the service on two devices at once without a paid plan unless you're storing a high volume of notes and syncing a lot of data. Ultimately, you may prefer to use something else, which is fine as long as it fits all of the criteria discussed here; however, in order to follow along with the book, go with Evernote for now (trust me and avoid the headache of painstaking research). Add it to the devices you most often use—I prefer to have it on my laptop and my phone.

If you're already using Evernote, clean it up; get rid of any notes or notebooks you no longer need, group notes logically, and add tags wherever appropriate.

Executor Insight

"I use Evernote...the goal is to keep everything out of your brain and in there. This is probably my most valued tool/strategy and has probably reduced my stress by 80%. Things will rarely slip through the cracks, and I can operate with a clear mind."

—Tim Zahodski
Artist Manager (Music Industry) | Interviewed in 2014

A Listing Tool

While Evernote *can* be used for lists and smaller bits of information, tools exist specifically to accommodate this need. Workflowy (WORKFLOWY.COM) is a tool I've used for years with great success and have shared with countless others. Like Evernote, it's accessible via a desktop app, mobile apps, and web browser, and it lets you structure information the way your mind works, whatever that may be. It lets you create and easily navigate through lists, with smaller lists nested infinitely within larger ones—exactly like the **Hierarchical Thought** model we discussed in *How?* When items are completed, you simply click a button that either hides or removes them. Some people prefer more polished tools like Google Keep (GOOGLE.COM/KEEP), but as of the time of this writing, I strongly recommend Workflowy, due not only to its direct applicability to the suggested mental model, but also due to its ease of use and beautiful simplicity. Other than a few optional keyboard shortcuts, there's almost nothing to learn.

Nearly everyone I've convinced to try Workflowy ended up a long-term user. If you pay for the professional subscription, you can create unlimited lists and take advantage of features such as automated daily backups, custom themes, and more; however, you can perform most basic functionality with a free plan.

Remember our fictitious friend, Jackie? The whole-person hierarchy we developed for her can be represented perfectly in Workflowy. If you recall, at the highest level, her life was divided into two lists that represented the broadest practical way of splitting her focus:

- + Personal
- + Professional

By clicking the little + symbol next to each item, Workflowy lets you expand these top-level lists to see her life as a whole (we'll add a few more items now that you're familiar with **Scripts** and **Hot Lists**):

- − Personal
    - + *General* **Hot List**
    - + Parenting
    - + School
    - + DJ/Music
    - + Health and fitness
- − Professional
    - + *General work* **Script**

- + *Work* **Hot List**
- + Work meeting notes
- + Vacation/absence prep **Script**

By clicking on any item, you can see a distraction-free zoomed-in view of it. For example, clicking on the dot next to *Health and fitness* in the above list would show you deeper lists nested within it and hide everything else from view:

- – Health and fitness
  - + Soccer
  - + Gym

Then, clicking on *Soccer* would show you even further nested lists:

- – Soccer
  - + Soccer solo practice **Script**
  - + *Soccer* **Hot List**
  - + Stretches
  - + Ball control drills to work on

Then, you can expand these lists to navigate, as needed:

- – Soccer
  - – Soccer solo practice **Script**
    - Stretches (30 seconds each)
    - Practice each ball control drill (5 minutes each)
    - Address *Soccer* **Hot List**
  - – *Soccer* **Hot List**
    - Research a more challenging stretching routine
    - Inflate back-up ball (in the garage)
  - – Stretches
    - Shoulder extension
    - Rear hand clasp
    - Full squat

- Standing pike
- Kneeling lunge
- Lying twist
- – Ball control drills to work on
  - Happy feet
  - Toe touches
  - V-rolls
  - Pull-and-cuts

In this example, Jackie is looking at her *Soccer* lists and none of her other personal or professional lists, which lets her focus only on what she wants to focus on at the time. You can imagine that she's come upon a session of *Soccer* **Blocked Time** and finds herself out in her yard with the above series of lists pulled up on her mobile phone. She uses her **Script** to guide her and her other lists to provide the context needed to progress toward her goal.

The scale of perspective is completely up to her and easy to navigate, as it lets her zoom in and focus just like she does in her mind. I'm sure you can relate: you sometimes want to take inventory of entire undertakings, while at other times you surely want to focus only on the tasks at hand.

Listing Tools aren't just for lists, **Scripts**, and **Hot Lists**; I also suggest using a **Listing Tool** to record anything small. For example, I live just outside Philadelphia and spend a lot of time in the city, so the odds of my car being stolen at some point are pretty high.

I mean, I love Philly, but let's be honest about it.

Should my car be stolen, I'll need to provide information to the police. Unlike my chronically stressed-out friend, I don't have my VIN or license plate memorized; however, I can simply pull out my phone, go into Workflowy, go to my *Cars/automotive* list within my *Personal* list (which is actually a shared list with my wife's Workflowy account—another useful feature), click on the item for that specific car, and find the information there. I can also do that in a much easier way: I can search for the actual text included in the items themselves, like "car," "VIN," "license," or "license plate." My wife and I also share grocery lists, items to talk to our pediatrician about at our next visit, lists of healthy dinner ideas, etc.

Imagine that you're an employee at a mid-sized company. Take a look at a smallish bit of professional information that could be useful for you to keep in a **Listing Tool**.

- – Benefits Information
  - – Annual Bonus
    - 5% of annual salary
    - Split into two payments
    - 75% of bonus in first January paycheck; 25% of bonus in first July paycheck
  - – 401(k)
    - 3% is automatically deducted from every paycheck, matched by employer
  - – Health Benefits
    - Call advisor at 800-555-5555 or ask a question via online form on the company website
  - – Tuition Reimbursement
    - Up to $1,800/year
    - Must retain GPA above 3.0
    - See company website for details

This departs from the lists we've explored so far in several ways: items don't exist in a particular order, and they're informational as opposed to actionable. This list simply contains knowledge you would need to access from time to time, and it isn't lengthy or narrative enough to require a note.

Here's a simple **Script** example you might find in your **Listing Tool** within your *Work* heading:

- – Work Processes
  - – How to make a call to an outside line using the new phone system at work
    - Pick up the phone, press 99
    - Wait until the dial tone goes away
    - Press the squiggly arrow
    - Dial the number you want to call

Pause here and sign up for Workflowy if you haven't already. Again, you may ultimately prefer something else that meets all of the criteria I mentioned, represents **Hierarchical Thought** in a simple, navigable manner, and allows for the same ability to dynamically shift your view and focus. However, for now, sign up for Workflowy so you can follow along with the book. If you already use Workflowy, take some time to organize it and clean it up. You'll be utilizing a **Listing Tool** quite a bit throughout this book as you work through examples and begin to organize your goals. Once you're signed up, try to create a structure that reflects your life. Spend some time playing around with it and create some sample lists and sub-lists—**Hot Lists** for organizing tasks by theme and **Goal Scaffolds** to reflect some simple goals. Grab the mobile app and sign in there, too.

An interface like Workflowy's may be hard to get used to at first just because it gives you so much freedom, but after spending some time with it and curating it in a way that reflects your own mind and your own life, you'll find this to be an invaluable tool.

Some people like to keep their notes and lists in a single tool; I don't suggest doing so because each tool has its own strengths. Evernote allows for much more formatting flexibility (text markup, image insertion, tables, etc.), which can be handy for note-taking. On the other hand, Workflowy's (intentional) limitations force you to create pure, simple text content, and the flatter organizational structure (no notebooks, notes, etc.) make for more efficient searching and more direct parity to a whole-life hierarchy mental model. Beyond the tools' respective strengths, creating a firm distinction between lists and notes will help you keep both clean and well-organized, which will reinforce trust in the tools and encourage you to curate them properly.

A Calendar

Lastly, you need a **Calendar**. As of the time of this writing, Google Calendar (CALENDAR.GOOGLE.COM) is free and has every feature you should ever need. It's accessible through web browsers and easily integrated into the native **Calendar** apps on most phones and tablets. You can sync multiple Google **Calendars**, so you can see other peoples' changes in real time, as well as create, edit, and delete events within each **Calendar** from a single interface. For example, you may have a personal **Calendar**, your spouse may have a personal **Calendar**, your kids may have personal **Calendars**, and you may all share a "family" **Calendar**, which includes events you'll all have to attend. You may share yet other **Calendars** with friends or keep a separate professional **Calendar**.

Aside from keeping track of your commitments, **Calendars** also let you know when to begin and end sessions of **Blocked Time** relating to your **Have-to-Dos** and **Want-to-Dos**.

If you don't already use Google Calendar, stop now and sign up; all you need is a Google account, and you'll already have a **Calendar** available to you. Once you have an account, set it up to sync with your mobile device (instructions for your specific device are only a quick Internet search away). As with **Note-Taking** and **Listing Tools**, if you ultimately prefer a different **Calendar** tool, that's fine, as long as it fits the criteria mentioned and can sync across devices.

By this point, I'm going to assume you're willing to give these new **Behaviors** and **Traditions** a chance; now it's time to put your money where your mouth is. Open Google Calendar. Regardless of how you used your **Calendar** in the past, we're going to set it up so it directs virtually all of your waking time.

First, make sure your **Calendar** reflects your responsibilities as accurately as possible so you can fully trust it; this will let you confidently navigate around existing commitments when identifying opportunities for **Blocked Time**. This also reduces stress as it absolves you of the need to keep any obligations in your head. Don't be like my friend; get organized. Outsource your memory onto third-party tools.

Let's begin with your personal commitments. Add to your **Calendar** any gym time, dentist and doctor's appointments, events, parties, parent-teacher conferences, happy hours, sports practices, band practices, networking events, school concerts, sporting events, awkward first dates, amateur wrestling conventions, roller derby championships, pet massages, frat reunions, psychic readings, and cult mixers. If you already use a **Calendar**—and I sincerely hope you do—you probably have a good deal of these types of things in there already. Take the time now to add anything that may have been missed, tighten it up, and turn it into something you can truly trust to guide you.

Next, think about which events may be important to share with anyone with whom your life is intertwined. If possible, set up joint **Calendars** with these people. As an example: My wife doesn't use her personal **Calendar** quite the way I do, but we share two joint **Calendars** to which she contributes events and obligations. Even if she didn't reference them herself—which she does—she would keep them up to date because she knows and respects the fact that I rely on my **Calendar** as my source of truth.

Many professionals have their own work **Calendar**, often based in other tools like Microsoft Exchange or Google's G Suite. If you have a work **Calendar** that can be seen in your personal or combined **Calendar** view, feel free to make it visible, but make sure it still remains a separate **Calendar**. Don't start adding your personal events and obligations to your work **Calendar**, as many companies have policies restricting the use of work-provided resources for personal needs. More importantly, if you end up leaving the company unexpectedly, you'll lose all your personal events.

Notice that the specific tools suggested—for **Note-Taking Tools**, **Listing Tools**, and **Calendars**—all fulfill a set of simple criteria. They're all:

- *Quickly accessible* — They're all available on your mobile device, which you can pull out and access in a matter of seconds. If you're in a developed nation, there's a good chance your phone is on your person at almost all times, so it's by far the best place for **Execution Tools**. Even the most basic modern phones let you do much more than text and send memes to your friends.

- *Cross-device in real-time* — This is a way of saying that any update made on one device will be almost immediately available on another. For instance, if you make a change to Workflowy, Evernote, or Google Calendar on your computer, walk down the hall, and check your smartphone, you should see your change reflected there.

- *Redundant* — Redundancy is a technical term for data existing in more than one place, so if you lose or accidentally delete something, you can still recover it, either from backups, the cloud-based service itself, or from another device. Redundancy is one of the primary reasons I'm vehement about using digital technology for these tools. I've worked with people who carry around a single flash card for each day or who use sticky notes or small notebooks; while these **Behaviors** may work well for certain individuals, they're not redundant, and if you lose your physical notes/lists, they'll be lost forever. It's not 1989, so please don't do this. I can lose (or destroy) every device I own, buy new ones, sign into these services, and not a single note, list, or calendar event will have been lost.

- *Simple* — Each tool must be simple enough that you can master most major functionality after only a little use. If you use more complex tools with a whole suite of options, it will take you longer to feel like a power user, and you'll be less prone to use them or customize them in a way that suits your personal style.

You want to quickly cultivate a sense of familiarity with your **Execution Tools**, and using simple ones makes this easier.

- *Free* — While paid premium versions of Evernote and Workflowy exist, you can use most functionality with a free account. *Free* doesn't mean you should use it for years without putting money into the pockets of these tools' creators. It means there's no reason not to at least give them a try—there's no harm and no risk.

Recurring Tasks

You may encounter tasks you need to perform on a regular basis that are simple and don't necessarily fit into the **Hot List** model.

As an example, consider taking your car in for an oil change every few months. For most people, that's pretty isolated; such a task wouldn't be paired up with other, related ones, and since it's a **Recurring Task**, it wouldn't make sense in a **Hot List**. Since your car's health relies on this being done every few months, you can't let it lobby for priority against other tasks and risk being pushed down or chronically deferred. The best method for handling such a **Recurring Task** is to decide on **Blocked Time** during which you'll perform it, and create a recurring **Calendar** event for it. If a task is unavoidable, you may as well organize it to avoid losing track of it. Shed the stress of having to remember it—along with dozens of similar **Recurring Tasks**—in your head.

For instance, you could create an oil change **Calendar** event for 9 a.m. on the first Saturday of January, April, July, and October. You can also set reminders for one week before each so you can check your **Calendar** for any conflicts, adjust the times if necessary, call for appointments, etc.

Other examples of daily/weekly/semi-monthly **Recurring Tasks**:

- Take garbage and plastic/glass recycling to the curb every Wednesday night

- Mow the lawn every (or every other) weekend
- Refill your pill case or charge your hearing aid every Sunday
- Pick up your monthly public transit pass near the end of the month
- Meet a workout partner at the gym three times each week at a predetermined time

Sure, you'd probably remember to take the garbage to the curb without the **Calendar** event, but creating one eliminates the risk of losing track of the task on busy nights and then realizing once you're already comfy in bed. It eliminates the vague sense of responsibility that can—in conjunction with other undocumented obligations—add up to an amorphous undercurrent of stress. And what does it cost you? You perform the task and erase the reminder with the simple swipe of a thumb.

Do you take birth control or heart medicine at 8 a.m. each day? Put a recurring event in the **Calendar**. For things like this—when consistency matters—you can consider the event an insurance policy. Do you visit grandma and help her clean her house every Wednesday at 6PM? **Calendar**. Change the filter in the fish tank every Sunday? **Calendar**. Place your daughter's library book and Girl Scout uniform in her bookbag every Wednesday? **Calendar**. Personally, on the first of each month, I change my contact lenses, organize my home office, swap out my toothbrush, and perform about ten other small tasks.

Then, there are *yearly* **Recurring Tasks**. On November 15th of each year, I bring patio furniture into my garage, drain the hoses outside my house so they don't freeze during the winter, adjust my heater settings, and schedule time to have my gutters cleaned. I use a recurring **Calendar** event to remind myself that it's time to perform my *winter prep* **Script**, refer to it when the time comes, and work my way through it from top to bottom. I don't want to have to remember that stuff; I want tools to do it for me. I don't want to wake up in the middle of the night and realize I never drained the hoses.

Other examples of yearly or semi-yearly **Recurring Tasks**:

- Replace heater filters, clean the chimney, purge the water heater, etc.
- Organize tax and financial records and either file them with the IRS or send them to an accountant
- Update your résumé/CV just to keep it current and list recent accomplishments while they're still fresh in your mind, regardless of your employment situation
- Schedule doctor checkups, optometrist and dental appointments, etc.
- Perform spring cleaning

Unique Tasks

Unique Tasks are tasks that only occur once, and these too should be reflected in your **Calendar** when they're *time-specific* or *time-sensitive*. By nature, *time-specific* tasks are related to a time and, therefore, require very little thought. Consider *3 p.m. on June 4th: Doctor's appointment— bring referral*; this is a textbook commitment and aligns with how most people use **Calendars**.

However, if you find yourself with a time-sensitive task with no specific time assignment, you should assign it a time and put it in the **Calendar**, as well. Let's illustrate this with two examples.

Consider *Pick up football game tickets from Uncle Fred*. With something like this, you wouldn't just want to "try to remember to get to it before the game;" not only is it time-sensitive, but remember—you're trying to eliminate stress. Pick a time to do it and throw it in the **Calendar**. Even if you have to move it a little when the time comes, the task (and stress) of remembering is still outsourced.

By contrast, something like *Look into alternate Internet service providers* wouldn't be a good candidate for this practice since it isn't necessarily time-sensitive; instead, this one makes more sense as an item on a *General **Hot List*** and worked on when its **Priority** is appropriate during sessions of **Blocked Time** dedicated to that particular **Hot List**. Other priorities may bump it down, but unlike the *Pick up football game tickets from Uncle Fred* example, there isn't a specific time by which you need to perform this task before it's too late.

This all becomes natural with practice, and common sense will get you pretty far in assessing the best way to record, organize, and prioritize a given task. Either way, you're getting it; I can see it in your eyes. Get obnoxiously organized. Become your own personal assistant. Your own best employee. Your own overbearing, micromanaging project manager.

EXERCISES AND EXAMPLES

Let's perform a few quick exercises that will require you to use everything you've learned so far.

Writing a Collection of Short Stories

This will be your first time breaking a larger-scale goal down in detail.

Look at your **Calendar** and imagine that you want to write a collection of short stories based on events that occurred in your life when you were in elementary school. Writing a book is a lot of work (trust me), and you'll never get it done if you just *fit it in when you can*. That's an amateur mentality; you know ambiguity breeds failure. Imagine that you truly value writing this book and want to execute.

First, you'd want to come up with a **CMV** for this goal. Even though this is most likely not a real goal for you, as a thought exercise, take a few minutes and imagine what might drive you to pursue this, and craft a **CMV** from there. How would you word the **Mission**? What could you believe and what definitions of **Foundational Wealth** could drive you to want to create such a collection? What resulting end-state could you imagine wanting to bring to life by accomplishing this goal?

After this, come up with a realistic schedule for working on it. Look at your **Calendar** now; if this were a real goal, when would you dedicate **Blocked Time** to it? Pick a few recurring weekly sessions, log them in your **Calendar**, and continue on only once you've *taken* the time.

Yes—actually do this; you can erase them when you're done with this exercise. Stop looking at this page and do it. The actual, physical act of creating the event will help reinforce this mindset.

After performing any necessary research (an **Exploratory Phase**), you can create an **M-SMART Goal** that serves your **CMV**. Using your M-

SMART Goal as a guide, create a Script and Hot List for this project. This should take some time to do properly. Again, treat this like a real goal or project because this is practice for a skill you'll need when addressing any actual goals you may have—which, for all I know, could be far more complex than this example. Remember: your Script should reflect unchanging, ordered actions you take every time you begin a session of *Short story collection writing* Blocked Time, and your Hot List should consist of a Goal Scaffold outlining everything you need to do in order to accomplish your goal. When complete, your Goal Scaffold should read like a step-by-step instruction manual someone could follow to execute on this goal, and—if sufficiently detailed—your smallest Minor Tasks should each be individually actionable and feature clear completion criteria. As you perform research and begin writing, take advantage of your Note-Taking Tool.

If this were an actual goal, you'd want to share this goal with some family or friends—to let them know why you're pursuing it, and what days and times they can expect you to be off-limits due to Blocked Time commitments.

Even though there are almost endless ways to do this, here's one example: I'd personally block off time in the early mornings for this. I know if I really wanted to, I could block off some time on Tuesdays and Fridays from 6 to 7 a.m.

Let's look at my Script and Hot List.

Here's my Script, created in my Listing Tool. These are the steps I'd reliably traverse during every session of Blocked Time.

- Get into *writing mode*—this means I need to be alone in my home office or bedroom with Internet access disabled on my laptop and no other devices nearby; this also means my family needs to be aware that this is a *do not disturb* time
- Open my Note-Taking Tool and briefly review what I've written so far (if anything)

- Read a few paragraphs from one of my favorite authors for stylistic inspiration and to set the tone for the session
- Consult and make accessible all my notes related to this undertaking (in my **Note-Taking Tool**)
- Address my *Short story collection writing* **Hot List**
- Ensure all files have been backed up

And here's my **Goal Scaffold** in my *Short story collection writing* **Hot List** (also in my **Listing Tool**):

- Reminisce about elementary school and try to remember at least fifteen interesting stories.
    - Brainstorm: Did I break a bone? Make a friend in an unusual way? Discover music? Nervously try out for the soccer team? Experience my first romantic encounter?
    - Capture each as a two-sentence synopsis
- Narrow the list; select ten stories from the fifteen to pursue
- Decide on the order in which I'd like to write them
- Give each story a working title
- Create outlines for each story
- Write the stories
- Place the stories in an order that creates a good flow and overarching narrative
- Select a title for the collection
    - Assemble a list of five prospective titles
    - Do a quick Internet search to make sure the titles aren't taken; reduce the list based on availability
    - Decide on a final title
- Edit (for content)
- Step away for a full week
- Re-read the stories with a fresh perspective and perform a final edit (for content)
- Proofread and edit for grammar/spelling, etc.

Of course, if this were a real goal, writing a book would likely just be the beginning of the journey; it would most likely just be the first **Major Task** of a larger goal. I'd call it *Write the first draft* and, beyond that, I'd probably want to get it into the hands of people outside of family and friends, have it professionally edited, pursue a publishing channel, etc.

What did your **Hot List** look like? What did you do well? What could you have done better?

You can erase your **Script**, **Hot List**, and **Calendar** events for this example once you're finished, and then we'll go through a few additional examples to further reinforce this skill.

Reading More Consistently

Let's ease back a little bit and walk through a much simpler example. In keeping with a book theme, imagine that you've wanted to read more but haven't succeeded in doing so. Again, imagine a **CMV** for this; while a **Mission** for such a simple goal may be equally simple ("to read more consistently"), what could you believe and what definitions of **Foundational Wealth** could drive you to want to read more? What resulting end-state could you imagine wanting to bring to life by accomplishing this goal—especially one that's more of a lifestyle change than a goal with a clear end? What would an **M-SMART** goal look like?

Again, you need to identify and isolate some **Blocked Time** so you can protect this **Want-to-Do** from life's **Have-to-Dos**. *Take* the time. Do that now; create recurring **Calendar** events to reflect the times that would work for you if this were a real goal.

What times did you select?

Looking at my **Calendar** and trying not to use the same early morning schedule I used for the last example, I would block off two half-hour sessions each week: Tuesdays at 10 p.m. and Fridays at lunchtime.

With a **CMV** guiding you, create a **Hot List** for this goal. Given the nature of the goal itself, this would most likely consist of the book list you'd like to work your way through. You don't want to specifically call out the books you plan to read in the **Calendar** events themselves; the event titles should be something like *Blocked Time: Reading*, and the book list should exist in a *Books to read* **Hot List**. In order to create this **Hot List**, you can perform an **Exploratory Phase**, polling friends and family or searching online for recommendations.

When the **Calendar** beeps, and you know it's time to begin a session of **Blocked Time**, you can consult your *Books to read* **Hot List**; or, if you're mid-book, simply pick up the book you're currently reading.

Wait, where's the **Script**?

I'll leave it up to you. On one hand, reading is a simple enough endeavor that it most likely doesn't require a **Script**; in most cases, you simply need to *pick up where you left off on the last book you were reading*. On the other hand, you could argue that a **Script** could remind you to get your next book from the library or online store as you approach the end of the book you're currently reading. Furthermore, if specific rituals accompany your reading practice (such as drinking tea or seeking out a specific setting), a **Script** may help you reinforce peripheral **Behaviors** and, therefore, stay true to your commitment. Lastly, a **Script** would be critical if you were reviewing the books for a magazine, reading for a class, or otherwise taking notes about them because the undertaking would involve steps beyond simply reading.

Only you can decide if a **Script** would provide value or prove to be overkill in such a case.

When you finish a book, you should consult your *Books to read* **Hot List**, see where you left off, and pick up the next book on your list (with the highest-**Priority** book already at the top). Let's see what such a **Hot List** may look like:

- ~~Research and select books~~
- Read
    - ~~*Dune* — Frank Herbert~~
    - ~~*Emergency: This Book Will Save Your Life* — Neil Strauss~~
    - ~~*What We Talk About When We Talk About Love* — Raymond Carver~~
    - ~~*Mostly True: The Story of Bozo Texino* — Bill Daniel~~
    - *Contact* — Carl Sagan
    - *Labyrinths* — Jorge Luis Borges
    - *Gödel, Escher, Bach: An Eternal Golden Braid* — Douglas Hofstadter
    - *How to Be Good* — Nick Hornby
    - *Naked* — David Sedaris
    - *Consciousness: Confessions of a Romantic Reductionist* — Christof Koch
    - *Consider the Lobster* — David Foster Wallace
    - *The Man in the High Castle* — Philip K. Dick

In this case, for the sake of illustrating progress through the **Hot List**, there are items crossed off, but it's generally wise to keep your list clean by hiding or deleting completed items. Workflowy lets you do either. I'm personally a firm believer in deleting because I'm careful to be sure that a task is 100% completed (via **Test Cases**) before getting rid of it. Also, years upon years of hidden tasks can result in an overwhelming number of items, which is simply pointless; it's akin to throwing empty bottles in your basement "just in case you end up needing them again down the road." Like a bottle, the task did its job and no longer provides value. Don't be a task hoarder.

Do some research now, if necessary, and select a few books you'd like to read if this were a real goal.

Once you're finished, you should know *what* you're reading and *when* you're reading. In order to make this work, though, you'd next need to socialize this reading time and your intention to have it respected. If it applies to you, place the **Blocked Time** event in joint or family **Calendars** and consider who you'd have to speak with about it. What would you say?

Building a Robot

Lastly, let's break down a much more complex, long-term goal in extreme detail. In doing so, we'll highlight some critical details yet unexplored.

Imagine that you'd like to build a robot. Assuming you have no background in computer science, robotics, or electrical or mechanical engineering, you're starting this adventure from scratch, so this is going to be a challenge. Where do you begin?

With your definitions of **Foundational Wealth** providing large-scale perspective and boundaries, you'll need to first construct a **CMV** to *define* your intention. Come up with a **CMV** for this goal now; articulate the **Values** you want to address (**Credo**), and then from it, craft your aspiration (**Mission**) and illustrate a success state (**Vision**). Even though it's fictitious, you can imagine, for instance, that you've recently married and would like to bond with your new stepson, who's a budding robotics aficionado. Or, if you'd like to flex your imagination a bit more, imagine that you'd like to start a robotics company because you want to help people with disabilities perform everyday tasks; that you believe that specialized assistive robotics is going to be a near-future boom industry; and that your image of success involves watching someone unable to use their hands successfully traverse daily challenges through products your company built. Imagine that you believe that in order to found such a company, you'll need to understand robotics much more deeply than you currently do.

Once you're finished crafting your **CMV**, you can build an **M-SMART Goal** (*refine* your intention). What's your motivation? What's your loose timeline? What are good success criteria? What would you like the robot to minimally do?

111

An **M-SMART Goal** could be: *I want to build a robot that can pick up a full glass of water, move it a few meters away, and place it down (unbroken and unspilled) before February 28th three years from now. I believe in the value of assistive robotics, and believe this technology will be transformative for society and the economy. I want to be involved in this transformation, and I believe that building a robot on my own is an immersive first step toward familiarizing myself with this exciting world.*

Let's break it down.

- It's *motivation-focused* — You clearly summarized your motivation for taking on the goal—and did so on three levels:
  1. Your motivation for selecting the goal's general domain: *I believe in the value of assistive robotics, and believe this technology will be transformative for society and the economy.*
  2. Your personal motivation for engaging in the goal: *I want to be involved in this transformation.*
  3. Your motivation for performing this specific goal (as opposed to other goals that may help service your larger goal): *I believe that building a robot on my own is an immersive first step toward familiarizing myself with this exciting world.*
- It's *specific* — You didn't say *build something*, but rather *build a robot*. You didn't say *that does something cool*, but rather specified the *glass of water* task.
- It's *measurable* — The ultimate success criterion is the ability to perform the *unbroken, unspilled glass of water* task. Once complete, your creation will either pass or fail.
- It's *attainable* — Your goal isn't to *build a robot that can jump across the Grand Canyon*. Some simple initial research will show you that robots can be built to perform tasks like *moving a glass of water*, and things like that have certainly been built in the past—even by amateurs and hobbyists—with great success.

- It's *realistic* — A person of average intelligence could realistically gain the skills necessary to build this type of robot within three years if they studied and worked hard.
- It's *time-bound* — You picked a distinct end date by which you'd like to reach your goal.

Once you have an **M-SMART Goal**, you'll need to begin drafting an execution plan. This should prompt you to allocate regular sessions of **Blocked Time** for your robot-building project, making sure to dedicate to it enough weekly time to hit your newly minted deadlines. This should also prompt you to create a **Script** that details the process you follow each and every time you encounter a session of **Blocked Time**. While you haven't embarked on an **Exploratory Phase** yet, you can imagine some basic actions you can take to structure each session, and then adjust your **Script** once you better understand the goal. As early as possible in this process, work to socialize your plan and ensure you're building the **Culture** necessary to support it.

Next, begin building your **Hot List/Goal Scaffold**. First, come up with a list of logical top-level **Major Tasks**. How would you break this down? Here's one example:

- Exploratory Phase
- Learn how to build robots
- Learn how to program robots
- Build a test robot
- Build the water-moving robot

Your **Exploratory Phase** should always take place early in the process because it will help you refine your tasks and adjust your scope and target timelines.

Note that I included the **Major Task**, *Build a test robot*, and by now you should know why. The last phase of your plan will involve building the robot you'd ultimately like to create; however, before doing so, you're probably going to want to build at least one less-sophisticated robot in order to develop the skills necessary for your final project, get beginner mistakes out of the way, and gain a better understanding of what success will look like for your final robot.

As discussed, don't skip **Building a Body of Work** tasks. If you do, your final robot will suffer, and you'll do a disservice to your **Mission**. You won't delay your final goal achievement as drastically as you think you will. You're now far more organized and intentional than you've been, and these tasks will help you develop skills and predict challenges more readily when you build your final robot.

Now that you've articulated the goal as four **Major Tasks** (plus an **Exploratory Phase**), you can create a more detailed **Goal Scaffold**, breaking down each **Major Task** into **Minor Tasks**. For example, the first **Major Task**, *Learn how to build robots*, can be broken down as follows:

- Learn how to build robots
    - Spend time researching general robotics and electrical engineering; begin with Wikipedia and YouTube beginner robot tutorials; take notes
    - Read *Robot Builder's Bonanza, 4th Edition*, by Gordon McComb
    - Complete at least four of the rudimentary robotics projects outlined in the above book

Note that I didn't just know about the above book off the top of my head; I researched it during the **Exploratory Phase**.

With the first **Major Task** broken down, it's time to address the others. Again, in a real scenario, you'd spend a lot of time performing online research to understand what each **Major Task** should entail. For now, though, here's an example of one possible breakdown of the **Major Task**, *Build a test robot*:

114

- Build a test robot
  - Create rough designs
  - Research materials
  - Adjust designs
  - Purchase materials
  - Build robot
  - Program robot
  - Test robot
  - Make pertinent adjustments

Each of these can be further broken down into even more granular, independently actionable **Minor Tasks**. For instance, the *Build robot* task itself involves building multiple different parts separately—the chassis and the functional inner workings—and these, in turn, should be comprised of multiple **Minor Tasks** that are performed in a sensible order.

You know what your (loose) overall robot-building deadline is, as you defined it in your **M-SMART Goal**; now it's time to fit your **Goal Scaffold** into this time frame and decide on date ranges for each **Major Task**. The goal of this exercise is to come up with realistic timelines that will ensure consistent progress by applying reasonable positive pressure while still accounting for the possibility of unexpected hiccups. There's an art to balancing the two, and both overly forgiving and unrealistic, high-pressure commitments reduce engagement.

Let's talk about timelines in detail.

Much like most of us are used to loosely defined goals, the idea of applying timelines to personal projects of any sort may seem foreign. What's more, in many professional contexts—a domain in which timelines have long been the norm—they've in many ways become a thing of the past. Over the past few decades, "agile" methodologies like Scrum and Kanban have replaced traditional project-management processes in the workplace, and most businesses that have embraced them would likely claim they've provided immense value.

However, there's a place for timelines. While I don't use them for most things, they're a critical aspect of the goals I hold most dear—the ones I can't afford to let fail. Let's apply timelines to the current example, and in doing so, we'll discuss them a bit more.

Let's imagine today is January 1, 2020 (for the sake of a nice, round number). Take a look at our **Major Tasks** and their timelines:

- Learn how to build robots [Jan. 1, 2020–Oct. 31, 2021]
- Learn how to program robots [Nov. 1, 2021–Apr. 30, 2022]
- Build a test robot [May 1–Sept. 30, 2022]
- Build the water-moving robot [Oct. 1, 2022–Feb. 28, 2023]

Now, let's apply timelines to each **Minor Task** associated with one of the above **Major Tasks**.

- Learn how to build robots [Jan. 1, 2020–Oct. 31, 2021]
    - Spend time researching general robotics and electrical engineering; begin with Wikipedia and YouTube beginner robot tutorials; take notes [Jan. 1–June 31, 2020]
    - Read *Robot Builder's Bonanza, 4th Edition*, by Gordon McComb [July 1, 2020–March 31, 2021]
    - Complete at least four of the rudimentary robotics project outlined in the above book [Apr. 1–Oct. 31, 2021]

This illustrates an option you face. You can:

- Use your overall project deadline to determine timelines for your **Major Tasks** and then fit the timelines of your **Minor Tasks** into them

    Or

- Take your first **Major Task**, decide on timelines for each of its **Minor Tasks** in order, and then use the start date of the first **Minor Task** and the completion date of the final **Minor Task** to define the timeline of the parent **Major Task**. Once you've done this for all **Major Tasks**, you'll have determined the time boundaries of your overall **M-SMART Goal** and can adjust it accordingly.

Which method you choose is ultimately up to you and should make sense given the complexity of the project. For simple goals, the former usually works well, as it's easier to adjust the **Major** and **Minor Tasks** in minor ways that require little change to your **M-SMART Goal** time commitment. For more complex goals, however, I suggest the latter— start by applying timelines to the smallest **Minor Tasks** and traversing the **Goal Scaffold** hierarchy upward toward the largest **Major Tasks**. After doing so, you'll understand the goal much better than you did when initially defining it, and if your initial target timeline turns out to be unrealistic, you can adjust it before you begin.

This second method also provides you with a good opportunity to audit your goal. If the initial deadline you committed to in your **M-SMART Goal** is *drastically* different from the one you ended up with after breaking it down, you should ask yourself if the broken-down goal has grown too much—if it's become too ambitious or inclusive—and if it still serves your **CMV** in its new, refined state. Pare it down as much as possible. Likewise, after breaking down your goal in detail, you may discover that your initial **M-SMART Goal** was perhaps too narrow in scope. With time and practice, you'll learn to create harmony between your initial loose time commitment and the timelines affixed to your **Major** and **Minor Tasks**.

However, you should, in most cases, avoid applying timelines to your most granular **Minor Tasks**. In this example, *Spend time researching general robotics and electrical engineering* has a six-month timeline associated with it. It should be comprised of a series of more granular, actionable **Minor Tasks**, citing specific articles and tutorials—but would it be valuable to apply timelines to those **Minor Tasks**?

There's no steadfast rule here, and the answer lies at the intersection of your specific preferences and tendencies, and what **Behaviors** and **Traditions** you need to adopt in order to circumvent your less-productive attributes. Let's illustrate this with a slightly simpler example. Consider the following **Goal Scaffold**:

- Turn the basement closet into a vocal booth for a home recording studio
  - Research equipment
  - Demolish closet
  - Rebuild closet as a vocal booth
  - Etc.

After an **Exploratory Phase**, you may very well end up the following realistic timelines:

- Turn the basement closet into a vocal booth for a home recording studio
  - Research equipment [Jan. 1–Jan. 15]
  - Demolish closet [Jan. 15–Jan. 31]
  - Rebuild closet as a vocal booth [Feb. 1–Mar. 15]
  - Etc.

Within these **Major Tasks**, you may have worked out the following details:

- Turn the basement closet into a vocal booth for a home recording studio
  - Research equipment [Jan. 1–Jan. 15]
    - Microphones and stands
    - Headphones
    - Wiring

- Soundproofing insulation
  - Demolish closet [Jan. 15–Jan. 31]
    - Tear out existing walls
    - Dispose of waste
    - Clean
  - Rebuild closet as a vocal booth [Feb. 1–Mar. 15]
    - (and so on…)
  - (and so on…)

Does it make sense to apply timelines to each individual **Minor Task** within *Research equipment*? If you did, it could end up looking like this:

- Turn the basement closet into a vocal booth for a home recording studio
  - Research equipment [Jan. 1–Jan. 15]
    - Microphones and stands [Jan. 1–Jan. 4]
    - Headphones [Jan. 5–Jan. 8]
    - Wiring [Jan. 9–Jan. 11]
    - Soundproofing insulation [Jan. 12–Jan. 15]

For some, this level of granularity helps prevent a natural tendency to fall into cycles of procrastination. For others, overly granular timelines could turn otherwise-innocuous hiccups into time and energy wasted reapplying timelines to your tasks. Imagine that you had to deal with an unexpected family situation from January 1st through January 3rd; if the timeline was only affixed to *Research equipment*, you could still likely complete all of the **Minor Tasks** that comprise it within the time frame allotted by working a bit harder and faster than planned. However, if you had affixed timelines to the most granular **Minor Tasks**, you'd now have to adjust the timelines on four different tasks; and in more extreme cases, this could also cause the need to adjust **Minor Task** timelines across multiple **Major Tasks**, and so on and so forth.

In short: use your head. Know yourself. Learn and adjust your **Behaviors** as you become used to this framework, and customize it to fit your personal style. I personally tend to apply timelines to tasks one level above the most granular and bake in a reasonable amount of buffer time.

Do you see what I mean when I say you should act like a project manager for your own life and goals? Project managers break large initiatives down into collections of manageable, actionable tasks. They construct deadlines, which give them the tools and context to enforce focus and communicate progress (or lack thereof). That's no different from what you're being asked to do here.

Again, all of this may seem like a lot of work, but formulating and following a detailed plan always outperforms *winging it*; you'll lessen frustration and confusion, and you'll be far less likely to give up on your goal. Ambiguity in any form reduces engagement and exacerbates frustration. By the time you finish building and applying timelines to a **Goal Scaffold**, you should have before you a crystal-clear outline detailing every small step from where you are to where you want to be— your **Mission** fulfilled and your **Vision** a reality—and clear expectations about when you plan to get there. There have been times when I've finished constructing a **Goal Scaffold**, stepped back, and taken a moment to simply relish the significance: I had before me a customized, step-by-step instruction manual for reaching my goal. What more could you ask for?

Next, you'll become familiar with the third and final **Foundation of Execution**, but this has been a lot to take in, so while you can continue reading, I suggest you spend the next week settling into this new way of operating. Use the **Execution Tools** you've adopted. Manage complexity in every aspect of your life. Be strict. Only with time spent constantly ingraining these **Behaviors** and **Traditions** will they cease to be something you need to consciously think about. Anything can become habitual through immersion. Get used to referencing your **Calendar** as the primary source of truth when it comes to your responsibilities and availability. Get used to seeing **Blocked Time** on your **Calendar** and respecting it.

Section off two half-hour sessions of **Blocked Time** this week for something—it doesn't matter what it is for now. Meditation. Reading. Playing the flute. Building model trains. Giving your ferret a pedicure. Get used to how it feels to *take* time instead of constantly trying to *find* time. Get used to being strict about starting and stopping on time. Get used to a new world where order defines your **Personal Culture's Behaviors** and **Traditions**.

A word of advice: If you're like many with whom I've shared this method, you may be riding a wave of enthusiasm right now, and it may be tempting to block off hours upon hours each day. While I appreciate that, it's most likely not realistic, and even if you somehow actually have multiple hours to kill each day, you'll burn out if you start off too aggressively. Ease your way in, get used to the tools and the **Behaviors**, and prioritize the long-term value over the short-term motivation.

To summarize the second **Foundation of Execution**: *Take* **Blocked Time**. Arrive at the **Blocked Time**. Start on time. End on time. Treat the time with respect. Use your **Script**. Use your **Hot List**.

THE THIRD FOUNDATION OF EXECUTION: REMOVE FAILURE FROM THE EQUATION

Let's review where you stand:

By defining your **Foundational Wealth**, you've come to understand your overarching motivations and **Values**, and through this understanding, you're empowered to develop **CMVs** for any goal in your life that you value. You know how to use these **CMVs** as the foundations for detailed **M-SMART Goals**. You dedicate sessions of **Blocked Time** to your goals, think of complex undertakings through a lens of **Hierarchical Thought**, and know how to use **Scripts** and **Hot Lists** to organize the work involved and keep you on task during each session. Any complex goals are represented by meticulous **Goal Scaffolds** that both outline and detail not only the core steps required to execute on your primary goal, but also tasks related to **Building a Body of Work**. You know how to perform **Exploratory Phases** in order to truly understand and prepare to execute on your goals, and you appreciate the importance of treating **Blocked Time** with respect and socializing that respect. Through **The Franklin Principle**, you've made drastic fundamental changes to how you think about time and **Time Management**. You live and die by your **Calendar**.

(Cue inspiring music.)

You possess the knowledge, skills, and perspective necessary to use this repeatable framework to define, refine, and execute on goals of any sort (and help guide others who wish to do the same). You, my friend, are an organizational god. You're ready.

(Insert the sound of a record scratching.)

Not so fast. All of these wonderful **Behaviors** are going to go to waste if you fail, and you're probably going to fail. Sorry, but it's true. In fact, pretty much everyone fails at almost everything complex or difficult; that's why those who accomplish their goals (and especially those who *consistently* do so) are a celebrated minority in our society. With this reality in mind, if you'd really like to execute on your goals, reducing or removing the risk of failure is imperative. This is the true secret to guaranteed execution—and it's entirely possible—but it's going to require a somewhat drastic shift in **Personal Culture**.

That's a fancy way of saying, "This is going to get a little weird." You're going to implement some controversial **Behaviors** and **Traditions** that will force you to take an honest look at your goals, weed out the ones that truly don't matter, and surround the goals that *do* matter with a unique **Culture** that will force you to respect them in ways you never thought possible.

SEEK ACCOUNTABILITY. YOU'RE NOT ABOVE IT. REALLY.

By now, you already know how I feel about self-discipline. Traditionally, people believe the self-discipline required to execute should come from within; however, that model has a horrible track record. No matter how much you care about what you're doing, you're only human. Once you admit to yourself that you probably won't be able to *will* your goal's **Vision** into existence—and that you're not an exception—it's time to discuss practical tactics for keeping your eyes on the prize.

Accountability means expanding the scope of failure. It broadens the distress associated with inaction or failure because they cease to be private events; it exposes your desires and progress to others and subjects you to judgment.

Consider an example: a significant portion of the US population is clinically obese, and every year, millions of individuals commit to losing weight. The Internet alone provides access to abundant information about nutrition and exercise, much of which doesn't require a gym membership, unrealistic time commitments, or other challenging barriers to entry. Despite the availability of plentiful information and guidance, the majority of these individuals fail to lose weight each year.

How is it that so many are failing? Shouldn't you be able to simply make a decision, educate yourself with the free information available to you, and follow through?

When you make the decision to change something about yourself or your lifestyle, you're making a promise to *yourself* and holding *yourself* accountable; however, self-disappointment is relatively fleeting and painless. As with interruption and **Focus Rhythms**, you can take some pre-emptive steps and implement a framework that will make it easier to stay on track—in this case, by getting others involved.

When it comes to losing weight, it's not a coincidence that people tend to have more success with wellness programs than they do on their own. Sure, the information and resources provided are helpful, but they're often far from novel. The success of such programs is, in many cases, a product of the sense of community, support, encouragement, and **Accountability** they provide. There's value in exposing yourself to others; due to deep-rooted evolutionary factors, humans hate appearing stupid, weak, or flaky, so **Accountability**—which plays into these anxieties—is one of the greatest motivators in the world.

You probably already know this, but again, knowing is easy. It's time for action.

Within Your Circle

This is a classic and simple tactic: gain the support of someone you trust, whether that means a spouse, family member, coworker, or friend. Simply share with this individual what you plan to accomplish and why it means so much to you, and then ask for their engagement. You'd be surprised how much mileage you can get from this simple step. You employed this tactic at the very beginning of this book, and I use it all the time. Every single weekday morning, a close friend texts me a photo showing him running on a treadmill, and I have a weekly **Recurring Task** in my **Calendar** that reminds me to hassle him if he misses more than a day or two.

When you share your goal, be specific; cite dates (and your entire **M-SMART Goal**, if appropriate) and ask your support partner to check in on your progress at defined regular intervals. Especially for intensely personal or large scale, ambitious goals, exposing yourself and your vulnerabilities can be a bit unnerving, but adding even such a seemingly superficial level of **Accountability** to your goal can help you to trudge through the tougher times simply because you don't want to gain a reputation as someone who begins something ambitious and then fails to follow through.

Executor Insight

"There are thousands of reasons to abandon a project: no time, a sudden loss of drive...quitting is far easier than pulling through. To prevent the risk of flaking out, I often commit results to others. It makes me accountable publicly and deepens the meaning of what I do by including everyone."

—Gaël Blanchemain
Technologist/Minimalism Advocate | Interviewed in 2014

Beyond Your Circle

You can also leverage **Accountability** through more organized support relationships.

For well over a decade, I've met regularly with three like-minded and ambitious acquaintances to discuss our goals. This type of arrangement is a bit more involved than sharing your goals informally within your circle and requires a bit of work to set up; however, it can provide huge value. If such a setup seems like a fit, start with a simple three-step framework:

1. Choose a few people who are each working on something ambitious
2. Choose a monthly meeting time (over dinner is best)
3. Ask and answer three simple questions at each meeting

I've seen these types of arrangements called **Accountability** clubs, mastermind groups, goal buddies, and a slew of other names; I call it a **Flight Club**—a play on the secretive, exclusive gatherings from Chuck Palahniuk's book, *Fight Club*, and a reference to the idea that it helps ideas to *take flight*.

Hey, it's corny, but you'll remember it.

Why?

A **Flight Club** brings together like-minded individuals in a structured way, promotes growth and diverse perspectives, and, in many cases, eliminates any awkwardness that accompanies sharing goals with loved ones or requesting **Accountability** without reciprocation.

Who?

An ideal **Flight Club** should involve four people. Three can work, if necessary, but two is too few, and five is too many. Each individual should be involved in at least one ambitious project, goal, or undertaking.

You shouldn't be in a **Flight Club** with anyone you see socially on a regular basis (and certainly not close friends or spouses) because your **Flight Club** should be a sacred space with few connections to other facets of your life. You're going to need to be completely honest in providing your partners with uninhibited critical feedback, and you'll expect the same in return.

You should all live in the same region because you're going to have to meet in person regularly. I've seen this type of relationship work over video chat in a pinch, but such arrangements are far from ideal.

No outsiders or guests are allowed to attend.

Your **Flight Club** should consist of people whose opinions you trust—engaged individuals who will become truly invested in your success. These are your consultants. They should be individuals you would gladly pay to coach you; realistically, you *are* paying them for their services—not in dollars, but rather by returning the favor.

A poorly formed **Flight Club** involves people whose ambitions and challenges are:

- Too similar — Although four authors or four restaurateurs may seem appealing, diversity in experience gives rise to creative brainstorming and unexpected perspectives.
- Too dissimilar — If a **Flight Club** involved a philosophy doctoral candidate and someone who was trying to beat the world hot dog eating record, the participants may find it difficult to relate to one another or provide poignant advice.
- To dissimilar in scale — If a **Flight Club** involved the CEO of a multimillion-dollar company and someone who just opened a small shop in a strip mall, the flow of advice and mentorship may be a bit one-sided, and the more experienced individual may find it difficult to stay engaged over time.

My **Flight Club** includes individuals that fall right into the sweet spot. We face similar challenges—for instance, we all want to reach the next stages in our respective careers, gain experience, and provide value in authentic ways. We want to identify and follow through on networking opportunities. We want to navigate around and through professional conflicts, financial challenges, and creative blockages.

It can be difficult to locate the right people for your **Flight Club**—it's quite demanding, if you think about it: you need people you can trust but who aren't among your closest friends; they need to be local; and they need to be involved with ambitious goals similar in scale to your own but ideally not within the exact same domain or industry. I was lucky enough to form my **Flight Club** from people I'd already known for years (and we've since grown together), but if you aren't as lucky as I've been in this endeavor, take your search to the Internet. Browse online forums, groups, and communities dedicated to your interests or similar interests, and try to find people in your area that can fulfill this role for you. Share the idea behind **Flight Clubs** and present their value; remember, you're not asking for a *favor*, but rather providing them a service just as they're providing one for you.

When?

As mentioned, your **Flight Club** should ideally meet once per month. Leave plenty of time, and make sure no one has anywhere else to be immediately afterward. Don't meet more often than this, and certainly don't let more than two months go by without meeting.

Where?

Dinner in a restaurant is ideal, especially in a somewhat quiet place where you won't feel rushed. If you can afford it, it can be a good idea to meet somewhere a bit upscale. Your expectations and level of seriousness while sitting around in sweatpants are going to be much lower than they would be going out to a restaurant, and—in a *broken windows theory* kind of way—going to a nicer restaurant and making each meeting a bit of a special occasion will ensure you take the meeting seriously and treat the time with respect.

How?

Each meeting can open with casual conversation but should get down to business shortly thereafter—certainly by the time food arrives if you're meeting over dinner. Going around the table, each participant should answer three simple questions:

1. "What have I accomplished since last time?" — Everyone else should already know what you *promised* to accomplish (see Question #2).
2. "What do I want to accomplish for next time?" — The other participants should make sure you're not being overly ambitious or conservative.
3. "What advice do you have for me?" — Even though the members of the **Flight Club** are most likely working on vastly different goals, the perspectives of smart, passionate, invested people can be priceless.

Furthermore, no one should pick up their devices during the meeting except to take notes or add items to **Hot Lists**. At the end of the meeting, everyone should agree upon the time and place of the next one, and someone should be assigned the duty of sending out an email or text the week before the next meeting, reminding everyone of the time and place, as well as the promises each individual made last time.

You should think of these individuals as your support system, but you should still try to limit correspondence between meetings. If you truly have something that can't wait and need to reach out to your **Flight Club**, try your best to include everyone—use a conference call, group video chat, group text, or something of the like; no one should feel left out or as though their opinions are less valued than those of the other partners.

I can't tell you how much my **Flight Club** has helped me over the course of my career. They've kept me on track and focused, provided me with fantastic ideas, and—in more than one case—stopped me from making terrible decisions (for instance, when I thought it might be a good idea to pitch a 1,000+ page book). They've helped me refine goals, and their high standards have, in many cases, inspired me to execute at a pace and level of quality at the very boundaries of my comfort zone.

Look, I get it; this is the type of thing you read and agree is a good idea, but think is too much effort to actually pursue. You think you're an exception—as we all do—and that you can execute without doing

130

anything this drastic. Even if that's the case, the stronger your support system is, the better off you'll be. Invest the time and effort. Beyond the initial work involved in seeking out and setting up a **Flight Club**, it becomes a two-hours-per-month commitment. I'm willing to bet you can *take* the time.

Regardless of your preferred approach, take **Accountability** seriously and make it a core component of your goal execution framework. You should never be able to fail silently and privately; set yourself up for embarrassment in the eyes of people you respect. I'd personally suggest diversifying your **Accountability** portfolio by letting some friends and family know what you're working on, as well as setting up a **Flight Club**. In addition, I encourage you to explore other options for tapping into external **Accountability**; there are an array of online services, apps, and communities dedicated to this. As of the time of this writing, *Stikk* remains one of the more popular purveyors of said services; founded by a team of decorated academic economists, *Stikk*'s platform not only provides a framework for community support, but it lets users put money on the line.

This provides a perfect segue into our next topic. While **Accountability** certainly makes inaction or failure more difficult on its own, it also serves as the foundation of the next tool in your arsenal—the tactic that *truly* takes failure out of the equation.

THE SECRET WEAPON: EMPLOY TACTICAL CONSEQUENCES

In setting up an **Accountability** framework, you've learned to broaden the distress associated with inaction or failure. Now it's time to take things to the next level. In the introduction to this **Foundation of Execution**, I mentioned that this is going to get a little weird; here's where that happens.

In exploring the idea of **Accountability**, we used the example of obesity in the United States—we'll continue with that theme in order to introduce the idea of **Tactical Consequences**. Imagine for a moment that you'd like to lose some body fat. You may decide to eat healthfully and head to the gym each morning. You use the principles and **Behaviors** taught in this book to ensure you have everything needed to execute— you confront your motivations; create a **CMV** that illustrates a success state and articulates how your weight is robbing you of things you value; craft an **M-SMART Goal**; build **Scripts** to guide your morning routine and exercise sessions; go through a proper **Exploratory Phase** to educate yourself on exercise and nutrition approaches; use a **Listing Tool** to organize everything from grocery lists to exercise plans; keep a progress journal in your **Note-Taking Tool**; leverage **Accountability** by telling some friends about your plans and urging them to check in on your progress, and so on.

Good work!

However, when you resolve to do something, you're at one point in your life (let's call it *Point A*). The next morning at 6 a.m., when it's cold and rainy and your alarm wakes you and reminds you to go to the gym, you're at a different point (let's call that *Point B*). Then, when you're at work and someone brings donuts in, you're at yet another point (*Point C*). Finally, when you're in a rush and hungry and pass a fast food restaurant with an empty drive-through lane, you're at another point (*Point D*).

These are four different people.

Who you are—your consciousness—is what many philosophers and neuroscientists refer to as *integrated*. You change as you receive and process new information, go through new experiences, and undergo fluctuations in hormone and chemical levels throughout the day. Since your consciousness—which is dynamic—is your sole connection to reality, *you're* dynamic. And while core aspects of your personality and memory forge a convincing semblance of continuity, you're constantly changing into what one could argue are fundamentally different individuals. Due to this, the *you* that makes a decision is a different person from the *you* who's tasked with enforcing it. More importantly, the *you* who's tasked with enforcing it is different from the *you* that will see the benefits (or lack thereof) down the road. When it comes time to do the hard work—to step on the treadmill at 6 a.m. or refrain from indulging in the donut—it's hard to imagine being the *you* down the road who would have benefitted from *current you's* sacrifice. This isn't nearly as much of an exaggeration as you may think it is, as science directly supports this perspective's functional validity. When we think of our future selves, our brains respond as though we're thinking of an entirely different person.[2]

You at *Point A* had the easiest job of all. Making a decision doesn't hurt; it's not work. However, in order to ensure you execute on *Point A you's* intentions, *Point A you*—honorable and idealistic, driven and clear-headed—needs to inflict your will on *Points B, C,* and *D you*. This is precisely what **Tactical Consequences** achieve.

---

[2] UCLA psychologist Hal Hershfield has done groundbreaking work on this topic.

http://www.anderson.ucla.edu/faculty-and-research/marketing/faculty/hershfield

Incidentally, a close friend actually *did* decide he wanted to lose weight a while ago and had failed at dieting and exercising for years. We were talking about it one night when I suggested a plan. The next time we were hanging out, he handed money over to a mutual friend and made sure I witnessed the exchange. We told our mutual friend that she was to return the money to him only if he had lost a predetermined amount of weight by a certain date. If not, she could keep the money.

Right there, we moved beyond simple accountability and implemented **Tactical Consequences**. The goal was weight loss; the method was handing over the money and agreeing to the terms; and the **Tactical Consequence** was losing the money. To be sure it would work, though, we made some additions that would cause additional distress:

- To his wallet — My friend was gainfully employed, so if the consequence was only five dollars, the risk of losing it most likely wouldn't generate proper incentive. It was important that he handed over enough money that it would be worth his while to follow through.
- To his sense of ethics — If he failed to lose the weight, he could take solace in the fact that the money was going to a close friend. I suggested that instead of keeping the money, our mutual friend should instead send it to a group or charity that supported a cause the dieter disagreed with. We settled on a group that it's pretty safe to say very few decent people would likely want to support (this is sometimes referred to as an *anti-charity*). Everyone agreed to the change, and my friend followed through on his goal for the first time since his first *Point A* years ago.

My friend was tired of *Point B* sabotaging him and making him look bad; it was time to wage war. He put his future self at risk of embarrassment and damage to his sense of integrity by sharing the goal with more people. He put his future self at risk of monetary penalty by putting money on the line. He put his future self at risk of indirectly supporting a cause with which both his current and future selves disagreed. He *tactically* subjected his future self to *consequences*.

We were certainly not innovators here. However implemented, the core concept is simple: replace self-discipline and motivation with consequences. Earlier, I mentioned that self-discipline and motivation fail to deliver consistent results, and now you understand why: they're fleeting because you're constantly transforming into different individuals. **Tactical Consequences** work because they transcend time: *inaction or failure become less likely options if they would introduce a problem to your life.* Set up your future self to fail at the cost of money, pride, possessions, integrity, or combinations thereof.

In some cases, due to the nature of your goal, you can put into place your own **Tactical Consequences** with little or no outside assistance. For example—and continuing with the ongoing weight-loss theme—during periods of my life in which I participated in martial arts competitions, whenever I wanted to lose a few pounds after the Thanksgiving/year-end holiday eating gauntlet (the goal), I would enter myself in a tournament a few weeks into the new year, but would do so in the weight class that contained my goal weight (the method); I would leverage **Accountability** by letting family and teammates know I entered, and then if I didn't make the weight, I'd face much stronger and larger opponents (**Tactical Consequences**).

As another example of self-inflicted **Tactical Consequences**, one of my closest friends maintained a day job for years while building his small business. Once it grew to the point that he could just about sustain his bills without working elsewhere, he pulled the trigger and quit (the method); if he didn't work hard to network and drum up new business, he would find himself in dire financial straits or have to again seek employment (the **Tactical Consequences**).

Let's discuss some implementation details and explore why it's important that you only use this **Behavior** sparingly.

Setting Mile Markers and Understanding Your Domain of Control

If your goal is long-term and large-scale, you shouldn't tie **Tactical Consequences** to the overall goal, but rather to **Mile Markers**— checkpoints of achievement that signify progress pertaining to your overall goal. Not only is this model practical because large goals are collections of smaller goals—as we saw when we broke them down into **Goal Scaffolds**—but there's also psychological factors at play. Hitting smaller goals and spreading your sense of achievement out over time will inspire you to continue more effectively than relying on a single, distant, long-term goal.

Goal Scaffolds, properly built, should provide a nearly perfect collection of **Mile Markers**.

Executor Insight

"Short-term goals breed long-term success. The thought of years of training can be a little intimidating. I know it was for me back in 2007 when I set my sights on the 2012 Paralympics. In order not to lose track of my ultimate goal, I set short-term goals along the way."

—Travis Pollen
Paralympic Swimmer, Personal Trainer, and Fitness Author |
Interviewed in 2014

Imagine that your goal was to become an accomplished glass artist. As mentioned, you wouldn't want to tie **Tactical Consequences** to the overall goal, but rather **Mile Markers** that comprise it. You may think that *winning a competition by a certain date* would be a good candidate, but it wouldn't be because such events are qualitatively judged by third parties; you'd be relying, in part, on the whims and biases of judges. Instead, tie the **Tactical Consequences** to things that reflect your own dedication to the goal, such as *entering a certain number of competitions before a certain date*. Doing so lies squarely within your **Domain of Control**, and the preparation required to compete will force you to adopt **Behaviors** that will ensure progress toward both winning competitions and your ultimate goal.

External factors can pose challenges and threaten your ability to execute on an **M-SMART Goal's** ultimate success criterion; while you can (and should) adjust for such challenges as they arise, you should tie **Tactical Consequences** to **Mile Markers** that rely entirely on your action or inaction. The simpler **Mile Markers** are, and the more they rely only on your own **Behaviors**, they more effective they'll generally be.

As another example (and harkening back to the writing/publishing theme we used previously), imagine that you wanted to publish a comic book. There are quite a few **Mile Markers** you could tie **Tactical Consequences** to surrounding writing, storyboarding, illustrating, coloring, etc., but when it comes to publishing, you're reliant on the willingness of a publisher to work with you. While you can *influence* that, you can't *control* it. Because of this, rather than setting a **Mile Marker** called *have comic book published*, pick something like *research and send well-constructed pitch letters to at least fifteen different agents or publishers*. When no one and nothing else can be blamed for your inability to execute on a **Mile Marker**, you'll find yourself robbed of excuses—that's an incredibly freeing feeling and lets you define **Tactical Consequences** with impunity.

Which brings us to the next topic…

Taking It to the Limit

Approach the following first as a philosophical exercise before worrying about implementation:

The **Tactical Consequences** tied to **Mile Markers** for your goal that lie within your **Domain of Control** should be extreme if the goal is incredibly important to you. Remember: *inaction or failure become less likely options if they would introduce a problem to your life*. Let's amend that to say *a catastrophic* problem because the *more* extreme the consequences, the *less* likely you are to tolerate failure as an option.

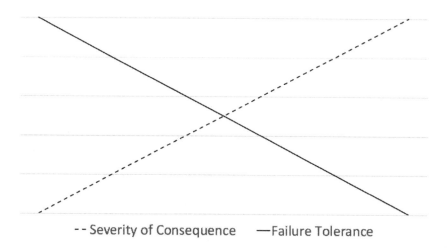

-- Severity of Consequence   —Failure Tolerance

As consequences approach *intolerable*, inaction or failure becomes almost *impossible*. You at *Point A*—the enthusiastic, driven version of you—has the potential to become an asshole. A sadistic, devious villain. In such cases, *Point B you* may hate the *Point A* version, but too bad—*Point A you* is in charge because they came first and have the intel needed to leverage *Point B you's* weaknesses, fears, desires, and anxieties. In accessing such intimate forces, you can all but guarantee a degree of success otherwise virtually unattainable.

It's difficult to come up with extreme **Tactical Consequence** examples because the aforementioned weaknesses, fears, desires, and anxieties are different for everyone. For some, social consequences are far more painful than monetary ones. For some, denial of creature comforts may be a big driver. Be honest with yourself and push the boundaries. If you love television, banning yourself from watching it for a month may seem like a good **Tactical Consequence**, but does it *guarantee* you'll follow through on your **Mile Markers**? What about if you banned all television and films for a year, and would have to destroy your television?

This illustrates a point: every goal comes with the opportunity to ask yourself if you value success/execution relating to your goal—and all it will bring you—more than you value the things you choose put on the line. Think of your motivations—the **M** in your **M-SMART Goal**—and know that if you want to *guarantee* success, you always have the option of taking it far, digging deep, and making it hurt.

Before you dismiss me as a lunatic, consider that *me at Point B* can be pretty lazy. *Me at Point C* can be afraid of failure. *Me at Point D* can be overwhelmed by life's responsibilities, and—worst of all—*me at Point E* can decide my goal simply didn't matter in the first place. I know I'm as weak-willed, fickle, and easily distracted as anyone else, so for the goals I've valued the most, I've devised quite a few extreme **Tactical Consequences** over the years.

When you began this book, I promised you the ability to take failure out of the equation—to entirely remove inaction and failure as options. This is it—this is how. It's not complex, but it's something very few have the guts to discuss honestly because we secretly like the failure option; it comforts us. We like being able to lay blame on external forces, or to be able to shrug off a previous goal as a phase or bad idea. We like the eject button the failure option provides. I also believe—deep down in our hearts—we all know it's possible to remove failure. You *would* hit that first fitness **Mile Marker** if failing to do so meant using up your vacation time jogging across your entire state in the winter. You *would* hit your first side-business **Mile Marker** if doing so prevented your grandmother from opening a sealed envelope containing a detailed list of embarrassing secrets. You *would* finish the first draft of that screenplay if you would have to donate your car if you missed your deadline. You *would* launch that online store in time if failing to do so meant burning every existing photo of your beloved childhood pet and deleting any digital copies. It's a weird and ugly concept, but you should keep it in mind as a viable option because it works when nothing else will. When you've failed, procrastinated, and made excuses for years. And when the goal truly matters, I urge you to push the boundaries because *if you can tolerate the consequence, inaction and failure will always be options.*

Setting **Mile Markers** well within your **Domain of Control** gives you the freedom to craft **Tactical Consequences** that are as ruthless, life-altering, reputation-damaging, and police-report-filing as you'd like. Remember, this is you at *Point A*; the **Accountability** and **Tactical Consequences** you bring to this goal will force you to push through when (not *if*) you lose steam at *Point B, C*, or beyond.

Now that you understand that this option is available to you, you need to understand how to wield it responsibly.

Extreme Tactical Consequences as a Filtration Tool

At this point, you may be under the impression that I'm constantly setting up booby traps for myself, living a high-stakes life wrought with minute-by-minute drama and self-abusive consequences. This is certainly not the case, and if I don't make it to the gym on time today, I can assure you I won't have to burn my house to the ground. Quite the opposite; **Tactical Consequences** are an incredibly powerful tool that should be used with caution, and not every goal warrants them. In fact, the exercise of applying **Tactical Consequences** can often transform into an exercise in filtration.

Earlier, I explained how you alone define which **Behaviors** are rewarded and celebrated and which aren't tolerated in your **Personal Culture**. By implementing **Tactical Consequences** (a **Behavior**), you demonstrate that inaction or failure relating to *goals you value* isn't tolerated, and if you aren't willing to commit distressing **Tactical Consequences** to a goal, then you have to ask yourself if you really want to achieve it as badly as you claim. That's vital and healthy; if you're an excitable, enthusiastic dreamer who is interested in taking on the world and chronically spreading yourself thin, the threat of an extreme **Tactical Consequence** forces you to reconsider, reduce scope, prioritize, and focus your energy. In many cases, the internal discussion about whether or not a goal is truly important enough to decorate with extreme **Tactical Consequences** frees you; it forces you to ask if the goal was an empowering fantasy you've always held onto for comfort but never truly wanted. It isolates and assigns value to your *true* goals while weeding out the whims. It encourages you to weigh a goal against its ability to bring you more **Foundational Wealth**.

This doesn't mean you shouldn't pursue goals that you value but to which you can't justify applying **Tactical Consequences**. Personally, I dedicate sessions of **Blocked Time** to a number of personal, professional, and fitness goals I value; I meticulously organize them with **Scripts** and **Hot Lists**, and have **CMVs** and **M-SMART Goals** crafted around them. I've even expanded the scope of failure by sharing some such goals with my family, colleagues, and—in certain cases—with my **Flight Club**. Without employing these **Behaviors**, I know I'm never going to progress as I'd like. While certainly important, these goals are far from my most vital; they don't have the potential to drastically change my life or help me accrue immense **Foundational Wealth**. For that reason, I choose not to tie **Tactical Consequences** to their **Mile Markers**. If I did so for every single such goal—especially if I made the **Tactical Consequences** extreme—I'd be a stressed-out lunatic. Not every goal is important enough to justify subjecting myself to this practice; and when one is, it's clear. I'm willing to bet you know which of your goals are worth subjecting yourself to risk and frustration, as well.

Think of **Tactical Consequences** as a potentially lethal weapon; respect them, use them sparingly and with careful consideration, and when you do actually deploy them, do so without mercy.

Defining an Executor of Consequences and Auditor

If I've convinced you that **Tactical Consequences** are an important tool, at this point, you may be asking how you're expected to make sure you go through with them. That's a great question; if *Point D you* can't be trusted to follow through on *Point A you*'s goal, they certainly can't be trusted to follow through on distressing **Tactical Consequences**.

Earlier, I cited examples that illustrate how you can often enforce your own **Tactical Consequences**—such as when I would enter martial arts tournaments in a different weight class, or when my friend quit his job in order to force himself to commit to his side gig. However, not every goal presents such an easy setup for **Tactical Consequences**, and this is where you may need to leverage **Accountability** in more unique ways. Online **Accountability** services like those mentioned earlier can often provide this for you, but may fall short when you want to venture into more extreme or unorthodox consequences. When it comes to such cases—depending on your situation, the nature of your goal, and interpersonal dynamics—you may be able to explore building a support team. Minimally, this means coordinating your goal/consequences with two individuals—an **Executor of Consequences** and an **Auditor**.

An **Executor of Consequences** is an individual who will remain actively engaged in your journey and up to date on your progress, and who will be willing to do the work to ensure that all **Tactical Consequences** are carried out. This is where you call upon your closest personal relationships or **Flight Club** participants.

This is also where things can become a bit uncomfortable.

However, true friendship isn't most evident in the currency of sympathy, but rather in respect for your best interests; love isn't demonstrated in leniency and concessions, but rather in helping you pursue and accrue **Foundational Wealth**. A true friend will force you to carry out **Tactical Consequences**—will refuse to come pick you up when it's cold, and your feet hurt, and you don't think you can run any farther. A true friend will deliver the envelope of embarrassing secrets to your grandmother. They'll come take your television off the wall and list it for sale online for you. And if the threat of a **Tactical Consequence** isn't enough to force you to execute on your **Mile Markers** when enthusiasm wanes, laziness kicks in, and interests shift, your desire to spare a friend from the uncomfortable position of having to enforce them may be.

The **Auditor** is a second individual—essentially a back-up or insurance policy—tasked with ensuring that the **Executor of Consequences** follows through on their duties. With this second team member in place, in order for a **Tactical Consequence** not to be carried out, *three* people have to fail to see the value in your success; *three* people have to make the decision to spare you the discomfort brought about by your inaction. At the risk of sounding callous, if you truly value your goal and openly share your motivations, yet you and your entire support system are unwilling to step up when the moment comes, you may want to reassess your character as well as the character of those whose company you keep.

If you have no family, friends, **Flight Club**, or network you can rely on, leverage online communities relating to your interest or goal domain. It may involve a good deal of work, but if you really want to do this, you can find a way to make it work.

Asking someone to be your **Executor of Consequences** or **Auditor** can be awkward; however, there are a few tactics you can use to make it less so:

- Increase buy-in by collaborating on **Tactical Consequences** — You should be the primary author of your **Tactical Consequences** since you're the only individual intimately familiar with the fears, anxieties, and desires from which they should be derived. However, if your **Executor** is somehow involved in crafting the **Tactical Consequences** and the details surrounding them, they'll most likely feel more of a sense of ownership surrounding enforcement.

- Make it fun — Don't approach the request from a place of seriousness, and don't make the task of enforcing **Tactical Consequences** seem dark and thankless. Embrace the unorthodox nature of the request, encourage absurd, funny, or embarrassing consequences, and—while your **Tactical Consequences** should cause you true distress when they relate to important goals—don't take yourself or this process too seriously. Don't be afraid to have fun with this.

- Don't withhold context — If you open up to someone and share your motivations and details surrounding struggles or pain you may have endured due to past failures relating to a particular goal, your **Executor** and **Auditor** will most likely feel a greater sense of responsibility to enforce the **Tactical Consequences**. They'll believe their enforcement will be in your best interests.

That's it for the third and final **Foundation of Execution**. I realize it may not have been exactly what you were expecting, but it's the truth: in order to follow through and execute, you don't need to be exceptionally intelligent, motivated, or self-disciplined. You simply need to create situations that force future versions of yourself to make decisions that align with your current **Values** and goals.

Before moving on, take some time to identify and write down ten or so **Tactical Consequences** that would cause you true distress—things you couldn't even fathom having to deal with. Be creative, and don't be afraid to get weird. Once you've done so, you'll have them available should you decide to employ them.

CONCLUSION

Not too long ago, you were thinking about reading this book. Of those who found themselves in the same situation, many undoubtedly decided not to commit the time and energy, and that's perfectly fine—I'm not personally offended (in fact, I'll never know). But that decision means their *human-against-self* stories are most likely going to continue on the way they always have. If they were considering reading this book because they were hoping to make strides in their career, they're most likely still exactly where they were. If they were trying to further their education, start a business, begin a creative endeavor, take their mental health more seriously, or even get in shape, there's a good chance they're continuing to relive a familiar cycle of self-promise and disappointment to this very day.

I wish them luck, and I sincerely hope they each eventually find their way to an approach that breaks that cycle.

Unlike these strangers, though, you turned off the path; you made an investment in *time*—your most valuable form of currency—that gave your story the chance to head in a drastically different direction. As simple as it may have been, that action showed that you believe in your story. You're now armed with everything you need to execute; you can apply sound execution **Behaviors** broadly to every aspect of your life, and you can turn any ambitious **Dream** into a true goal. Regardless of your motivations (and of how much work still lies ahead), congratulations are in order for taking the first step. Most people certainly don't make it this far.

REVIEW/SUMMARY AND THE PHILOSOPHY-STRATEGY-TACTICS MENTAL MODEL

While it wasn't called out overtly, this book was organized in a specific way; as we addressed the three **Foundations of Execution** in order, we did so from three perspectives:

- **Philosophy**: The broad, big-picture idea or reasoning behind the **Foundation**
- **Strategy**: The ways in which you give life to the **Foundation's Philosophy**
- **Tactics**: The detailed, granular actions you take to implement the **Foundation's Strategy**

This mental model transcends the contents of this book; it's a great way to conceptualize almost anything remotely complex—anything for which large-scale, sometimes abstract concepts result in (and are given life by) much smaller circumstances, events, and actions. If embraced and exercised to the extent of your imagination, it forces you to look at things holistically and with **Intentionality**; it prompts you to consider their origins, potential end states, and effects.

To illustrate this, consider an example: imagine that a country declares war on a neighbor. How could we look at this action from these three perspectives?

- **Philosophy:** The reason for declaring war
- **Strategy:** How/when/where to (and not to) engage the enemy
- **Tactics:** The individual actions that collectively comprise the narrative of the war. Examples: Utilizing a *pincer movement* to cut off enemy advancement when engaging on specific terrain;

having soldiers deployed to jungles pack extra socks to keep their feet dry and avoid debilitating conditions, such as trench foot; defending the road to a specific enemy stronghold using BGM-71 TOW missiles.

All three perspectives are valuable, as they represent the same concept (war) at three different scales, and if any one perspective is poorly addressed, you'll likely miss critical things. If you don't consider the **Philosophy** driving the conflicts (e.g., enemy state motivations; differences in **Values**), you may very well fail to predict enemy **Strategies** and, in doing so, employ incorrect **Strategies** to adequately thwart them. If you don't consider how/when/where to engage the enemy (**Strategy**), you may very well make mistakes in preparing personnel for the resulting battle locations (**Tactics**).

Given that you've learned quite a bit over the course of this short book, you may very well find it easier to retain, recall, and apply the **Foundations of Execution** to goals if you think of them through each of these three perspectives.

Foundation #1: Define and Refine Your Intentions

Philosophy

In order to execute on an ambitious goal or unfamiliar/challenging undertaking, you must approach it with **Intentionality**.

Strategy

In order to approach a goal with **Intentionality**, you must define it, refine it in extreme detail, intimately explore your motivations for pursuing it, and ensure those motivations are built into your tactical approach in ways that will keep them at the forefront of your mind.

Tactics

1. Before working to understand your motivations for pursuing any specific goals, first identify both self-focused and externally focused overarching definitions of **Foundational Wealth**, the currency—whether life or emotional experiences, material possessions, or anything else—that you value at the deepest level. These definitions will often help you understand your motivations across all aspects of your life and will, therefore, help you understand your motivations for pursuing specific goals.

2. Using your definitions of **Foundational Wealth** as a general guide, describe your goal in three ways: your **Credo** (beliefs about what is valuable, important, or desirable relating to the goal); your **Mission** (your purpose or calling relating to the goal; a manifestation of your **Credo**); and your **Vision** (an image of the **Mission** accomplished or being accomplished). The resulting three-perspective description is called a **CMV**.

3. Using your **CMV** as a guide, craft a concise, easy-to-articulate statement that describes your intentions in detail; this is called an **M-SMART Goal**. An **M-SMART Goal** is one that's Motivation-focused, Specific, Measurable, Attainable, Realistic, and Time-Bound.

4. Lastly, decide on the individual, actionable tasks required to execute on your **M-SMART Goal**. Spend some time learning about the nature of your goal in detail; the period during which this research takes place is referred to as the **Exploratory Phase**. With this information and your **M-SMART Goal** as a guide, create a **Goal Scaffold** in your **Listing Tool** that will serve as a step-by-step instruction manual detailing the actions you need to take to grow from your current state to the ideal end state— your **Mission** accomplished. When appropriate, be sure to include in your plan **Major** and **Minor Tasks** that reflect practice, learning, networking, experience, and credibility accrual; this is called **Building a Body of Work.**

Foundation #2: Manage Complexity

Philosophy

In order to execute on any ambitious goal or unfamiliar/challenging undertaking, you need to learn how to manage both the complexity that accompanies it and the complexity that's inherent in all aspects of your life.

Strategy

In order to manage complexity, you need to become and remain extremely organized and provide consistent structure across time, tasks, and tools. You can build an organizational framework by answering three questions:

- **How?** — *How* will you organize your goals?
- **When?** — *When* will you address your goals?
- **What?** — *What* tools will you use to record/represent your goals and the time you've committed to addressing them?

Tactics

1. The first step toward implementing the above **Strategy** involves deciding on a suite of **Execution Tools** you'll use. These tools are:

    - A **Note-Taking Tool**
    - A **Listing Tool**
    - A **Calendar**

    All three should be quickly accessible, cross-device in real-time, redundant, and simple to use.

2. A well-constructed complexity management framework should ensure no process, task, goal, or responsibility exists in your mind without representation in an **Execution Tool**. Use your **Listing Tool** to organize every endeavor you value—whether personal, professional, or creative—into **Scripts** and **Hot Lists**. A **Script** is a simple, static, and ordered process you follow to keep yourself on task when it's time to work on an undertaking; it applies a **Culture** of focus, seriousness, repeatable order, and consistency to the time you've dedicated to it. A **Hot List** is a dynamic, prioritized, and up-to-date list of the things you're actively working on; it should contain both *to-do*-style items and items to which you need to continue paying ongoing attention. Both **Scripts** and **Hot Lists** should be recorded in your **Listing Tool**, while longer notes (such as those you collect during any **Exploratory Phases**) should be recorded in your **Note-Taking Tool**.

3. Goals (or complex undertakings of any sort) should be captured in your **Listing Tool** and broken down into "**Major**" tasks, which are each further broken down into several smaller "**Minor**" independently actionable tasks. This conceptual structure is called a **Goal Scaffold**. A goal or undertaking's **Goal Scaffold** should read like a step-by-step instruction manual someone could follow to execute on it with minimal additional context.

4. **Time Management** should be approached from the perspective that time is a finite resource and a form of global currency: you can't *find* time or *make* time; you can only *take* existing time. **The Franklin Principle** states that *meticulously organizing the things you **have to do** lets you maximize uninterrupted time with which you can guiltlessly do what you **want to do***; this should inform how you think about how you spend your time and inspire painstaking time organization. Dedicate sessions of **Blocked Time** to your goal or undertaking, record them in a **Calendar**, and ensure these sessions are socialized and respected

by everyone they could impact. Never rely on motivation or self-discipline in order to remain productive and effective when working toward your goals; instead, take steps to reduce the risk of engaging in effectiveness- or productivity-eroding **Behaviors**. Begin each session of **Blocked Time** by ensuring you'll have minimal exposure to **Outgoing** and **Incoming Interruption**. Be realistic and honest about your attention span and split each session of **Blocked Time** between both active working time and time spent clearing your mind based on your ever-evolving thresholds for attention and mental fatigue (**Focus Rhythms**). When engaging in a session of **Blocked Time**, refer to your **Script** and **Hot List** for that particular goal or undertaking. This clear and repeatable system reduces complexity, ambiguity, and stress, and lets you execute on any goals or undertakings you've defined and refined via the first **Foundation of Execution**.

Foundation #3: Remove Failure from the Equation

Philosophy

In order to eliminate or reduce the likelihood that you'll fail to execute on an ambitious goal or unfamiliar/challenging undertaking, you need to increase or broaden the threat of distress associated with future inaction or failure.

Strategy

In order to increase or broaden the threat of distress associated with future inaction or failure, you need to build a framework of **Accountability** and employ **Tactical Consequences**.

Tactics

1. Socialize your goals so that inaction or failure will be apparent to those whose opinions you value. By leveraging **Accountability** and expanding the visible scope of failure in this way, you'll be better incentivized to execute on your goal (or the smaller **Mile Markers** that comprise it). You can socialize a goal by sharing your journey with family and friends, or by forming a more formal accountability support system (a **Flight Club**), with structured communication and collaboration protocols.

2. Set up an inactions-and-consequences framework around your goals so that failing to execute on either a goal or the smaller **Mile Markers** that comprise it results in distressing or negative future personal impacts (**Tactical Consequences**). The more extreme the consequences, the less inaction or failure become options, and as consequences approach intolerable, inaction or failure should become almost impossible. As unorthodox as this approach may seem, this is the single most important change you can make to reduce the risk of inaction or failure, as it circumvents facets of human nature that undermine your ability to consistently execute on your goals. **Tactical Consequences** should be deployed mercilessly but only for goals you feel are truly critical, and should only be tied to goals and **Mile Markers** over which you have complete power (your **Domain of Control**). If specific **Tactical Consequences** can't be enforced without third parties due to their nature, you can extend **Accountability** principles and enlist others (an **Executor of Consequences** and an **Auditor**) to help you.

CLOSING THOUGHTS

You're done. I'm proud of you. Before wrapping up, I want to leave you with a few thoughts that relate to execution.

Exercise Appropriate Agility

You've done an impressive amount of research. You have before you a **Hot List**, a beautiful **Goal Scaffold** containing a cascading array of articulate **Major** and **Minor Tasks**, and meticulously engineered timelines. And then, a few weeks into your project, you hit a hurdle. A roadblock. Something that forces your entire game plan to change.

Relax; this happens. I've been there. Life is a giant experiment, and as we venture into a new domain in which we are strangers—lost children in the dark—even the world's best mentors and **Exploratory Phases** can't completely eliminate *all* surprises. It's part of the fun.

When this happens, adjust—or, in the parlance of entrepreneurship, *pivot*. While your motivations and **CMV** should remain intact (and serve as the *North Star* by which you navigate any changes you need to make), your execution plan can change dramatically. To quote Bruce Lee, "be like water;" bend and adapt to accommodate the environment in which you find yourself. This is called **Agility**.

Let me provide you with an example of an *appropriate* adjustment: years ago, I co-founded a small financial technology startup. At one point, despite intense research, my partner and I discovered that a critical aspect of our business model wouldn't have worked because a type of digital transaction we needed to take place in a matter of seconds would have in fact taken weeks (and required an action on the behalf of the U.S. Securities and Exchange Commission). It wasn't easy, but we adjusted the business model to accommodate this problem and forged forward. As you can imagine, a few of our **Hot Lists** underwent quite a makeover.

This illustrates one of the reasons why it's so important to tie **Tactical Consequences** to **Mile Markers** over which you have direct control. In this case, had I tied them to larger aspects of the goal or actions or events that relied on other parties, I would have failed despite my best efforts.

In contrast, let me present a second example: imagine that you developed a new and innovative approach to yoga, and designed, built, and spent months trying to sell an online instructional course teaching it. Imagine that despite well-researched marketing efforts, your conversion rate (the percentage of website visitors *who actually purchase the product*) was low or nonexistent. In a case like this, you should, of course, work hard to adjust; among thousands of changes you could make, you could alter the marketing message in either subtle or drastic ways, try new sales channels, target a different audience, or alter the course to highlight your unique and differentiating approach. These would all be *appropriate* changes to your plan (**Appropriate Agility**).

Also imagine that your goal specifically involved creating an *online* course around your idea and that your **CMV** focused on themes like working from anywhere in the world and making your own schedule. Imagine that this goal represented a lifestyle and **Values** congruent with your definitions of **Foundational Wealth**—self-governance (part of your *self-focused* definition) and the opportunity to share your message with anyone across the globe, regardless of their location (part of your *effect-on-society* definition). In this case, deciding that the *online course* approach is a poor way to share your message, throwing away all of the work you invested in building the course, and pursuing more traditional means (like teaching in person at a local studio) would be an example of ***Inappropriate*** **Agility**. That would be fear taking you by the hand and leading you. That would be unwillingness to learn and grow through the gift of struggle.

To compromise on details large or small—to learn and grow in real time—is a fundamental execution **Behavior**; to compromise on your overarching **Mission** is to accept defeat.

154

Be willing to adjust but careful not to use **Agility** as an escape route. Use your head, honor your goals, and keep your **CMVs** and **M-SMART Goals** in mind with each decision you make.

Exercise Iterative Progress

You climbed Kangchenjunga. You became regional sales director. You can achieve Pungu Mayurasana. You published the book of poetry or released *Death Metal for Kids (Vol. 1)*. You were featured in the art show, completed radiology school as a single working mother, were featured on your favorite talk show as an expert in raccoon photography, or competed in *American Ninja Warrior*. Your waterproof vegan boomerang is selling exceptionally well online. Your doomsday cult just recruited its 10,000th devotee. I don't judge; your journey is your journey. Either way: *you did it*.

Now it's time to sit on the couch and await a peaceful and eventual death.

No?

In many cases, achievement as defined and refined in your **M-SMART Goal** may really just represent a step in what could ultimately be a grander plan. When you learned to create **Goal Scaffolds**, it might have seemed overwhelming to broaden your focus to include long-term considerations, but when your initial goal is nearing completion, it may be time to think about the future.

This could mean maintenance or further development (e.g., with fitness goals), leveraging your experience and networks to achieve further expertise or rise to greater challenges (e.g., with creative or academic goals), or expanding the scope of your influence (e.g., with personal brand or expertise goals). For entrepreneurial or financial goals, it could mean bold, exponential expansion. For professional goals, it could mean gaining better insight into the expectations associated with the next step in your career (even if that step is likely years away) and working to align yourself with those expectations.

It's time to gain celebrity endorsements for your waterproof vegan boomerang. It's time to take the doomsday cult international.

This could also mean reassessing or challenging your existing ideas about how you'd like your goal to interact with your life. While you should obey the wishes of *Point A you* and see your original goal through—and while your **M-SMART Goal** should remain untouched throughout the process of achieving your initial goal (barring extreme circumstances)—the exercise of deciding on next steps may furnish you with the opportunity to consider whether or not a long-term relationship with your goal makes sense. It could prompt you to consider whether your definitions of **Foundational Wealth** may have evolved since embarking on your original goal as a result of the insights, experiences, and growth provided by its pursuit. It may be necessary to construct a new **CMV** for this new phase; while your **Credo** should in many cases remain untouched (as your **Values** should often remain the same), the **Mission** and **Vision** for this new goal phase can often be different. Craft a new **M-SMART Goal** to describe this next phase and build a new **Script** and **Goal Scaffold** from scratch. Use the transition as an opportunity to audit your use of **Blocked Time** and **Accountability** frameworks, craft new **Tactical Consequences**, and—if utilized—bring your **Executor of Consequences** and **Auditor** up to speed. Basically, do everything you need to do in order to build another entirely new goal from scratch that represents the next phase of your initial goal.

Tactically, I recommend creating a **Major Task** near the end of each goal's **Scaffold** to represent brainstorming, defining, refining, and organizing the next phase.

You'll be able repeat these processes in this manner for as long as you like, and you can develop life-long goal journeys through these iterative **Behaviors**. Use your tools to reach the next landing on the mountain, take a breath, reassess the strategy for the next climb, and keep going.

Build Principles That Circumvent Your Shortcomings

Hedge-fund founder and self-made billionaire Ray Dalio once said that our principles are often born from our mistakes. While I believe that to be true for principles that arise naturally and reactionarily among the self-aware, I'd argue that there exists a second type: more *intentional* principles that are proactively crafted to respond to innate handicaps we need to circumvent.

For instance, I happen to be ambitious but scatterbrained, fickle, and easily distracted. It's a tragic mix. In order to execute on the goals to which my ambitions lead me, I needed to build principles that allowed me to circumvent these shortcomings. Luckily, I recognized them early enough in life that I saved myself from many of the headaches and heartaches that would have accompanied letting them lead to mistakes first and having to solve for them retroactively. In fact, the principles I adopted to circumvent these shortcomings in many ways led me to develop, test, and refine the **Strategies** and **Tactics** shared in this book.

What are *your* shortcomings? Be honest with yourself and try to understand what others see as your most execution-derailing traits; critical feedback from trusted individuals who respect your best interests should be a welcome gift. While you should work to fix them when possible, it's more important (and provides more *immediate* results) to determine ways to *work around them* so they don't impede your ability to pursue the things you value. This could mean utilizing **Strategies** and **Tactics** that prevent your shortcomings from having the power to affect your progress; focusing on endeavors that won't lead you to places where you're required to engage with your shortcomings whatsoever; or surrounding yourself with individuals who can fill gaps for you that you can't fill yourself.

Know your shortcomings intimately, let them be as much a part of your identity as your strengths, and approach them with **Intentionality**.

Work Opens the Door for Luck to Wander In

Luck exists; anyone who says otherwise is deluded. This fact is made abundantly clear in certain cases—such as the fact that some people will fall victim to illness, war, or other factors completely outside their control. But luck also exists on a smaller scale; for instance, there are times during which the needs of others coincide with your ability to deliver something that fills said needs. This applies to everything from goals and job prospects to romantic relationships.

Luck goes both ways: the right place/the right time and the wrong place/the wrong time.

However, consider the old adage, "luck favors the prepared." The work you do and the preparation to which you commit yourself ensure that you'll be able to capitalize on good luck or move on from bad luck when it befalls you. The examples are diverse and virtually endless. If you're personable, bold, and build and maintain strong networks (preparation), you'll hear about professional opportunities (good luck) sooner than others will. If you take care of yourself physically (preparation), you'll be more prone to overcome illness (bad luck) should it strike. If you perform a robust **Exploratory Phase** (preparation), you'll be able to adjust more quickly to unexpected and unavoidable changes that affect your goals (good or bad luck).

Whenever someone finds themselves armed with the suite of execution processes and **Behaviors** taught in this book, I urge them not to use bad luck as an excuse or good luck as an explanation. Work intelligently, and then take appropriate ownership of your failures and appropriate credit for your victories. Understand that luck is a part of life, and all you can do is prepare for risks and opportunities to the best of your ability.

Successful Individuals Tend to Share Two Specific Characteristics

Many will tell you that the smartest individuals tend to be the most successful, and I would argue that those who say that haven't spent a good deal of time with successful individuals.

Intelligence will rarely hurt you, but it's not an absolute requirement for success. Whether you think of success in the context of its intensely personal and wildly diverse **Foundational Success** definition or as a proxy for *consistent execution*, the massively successful disproportionately tend to be *tough* and *creative*.

You need to be *tough* because you'll fail. In some cases, you'll fail many, many times before you succeed. The weak give up, while the tough learn, adapt, and forge on. The tough accept criticism as a gift without unwarranted defensiveness. The tough feed off of challenges. The tough recognize their humanity—and the flaws to which that humanity gives rise—and make the difficult decisions necessary to circumvent them.

You need to be *creative* because creativity gives birth to interesting, innovative ideas, and when you fail (which is likely—see above), you'll need to come up with new and innovative ways to approach your goals. The best and boldest ideas—creative, personal, and professional—are often unorthodox, unexpected, and disruptive (born of creativity); they're also often poorly received or opposed at first (requiring toughness to persist through rejection).

I urge you to embrace your creativity and toughness and actively develop both, as neither are purely innate, and both can be developed. Surround yourself with people who exemplify and celebrate these attributes.

Don't Let Fear of Being Strange Limit Your Life

The Greek poet Archilochus once said that most individuals can be divided into two categories: foxes and hedgehogs. Foxes know quite a bit about a great many topics, and hedgehogs know almost everything there is to know about one specific topic—they dig deep (hence, the choice of animal) and attain expertise.

Does a less metaphorical term exist for foxes? The Cambridge Dictionary defines *dilettante* as "a person who is or seems to be interested in a subject, but whose understanding of it is not very deep." As victims of modern information overload and hopelessly damaged attention spans, many of us become interested in a broad range of varying topics and find ourselves becoming serial dilettantes. Hobby collectors. *Jacks of all trades, masters of none*, immersed superficially in dozens of pursuits but gaining mastery of none of them.

Let's be honest; we all know a few dilettantes.

The term *polymath*, however, is defined by the same source as "a person who knows a great deal about many different subjects." In popular usage, this also implies a person who possesses an array of different applicable skills or pursues a multitude of goals. A *Renaissance person*.

This type of fox sounds much better. Leonardo da Vinci was a successful inventor, artist, and scientist. Benjamin Franklin was—well, we don't have to list his accomplishments again. Nathan Myhrvold—aside from having a last name that could cause a teen spelling bee champion to lose bladder control onstage—is a renowned modern polymath with expertise in disciplines ranging from computer science (former Microsoft CTO), astrophysics, and economics to wildlife photography (winner of multiple awards) and barbeque (his team was crowned 1991 world champions). Brian May is an accomplished musician (guitarist for the classic rock band Queen), activist, and renowned Victorian stereo photography expert. Oh, and like Myhrvold, he's also an astrophysicist.

One of my favorite quotes, from science-fiction author Robert Heinlein, is, "A human being should be able to change a diaper, plan an invasion, butcher a hog, conn a ship, design a building, write a sonnet, balance accounts, build a wall, set a bone, comfort the dying, take orders, give orders, cooperate, act alone, solve equations, analyze a new problem, pitch manure, program a computer, cook a tasty meal, fight efficiently, and die gallantly. Specialization is for insects."

Celebrity examples aside, I've met polymaths in my own life, and I'm willing to bet you've met quite a few, as well. I'm also willing to bet they made quite an impression on you. These are the people I tend to admire most. In spending years picking their brains, I've found that while these individuals don't always learn *quickly*, they learn *passionately*. They learn *creatively*. They learn *daringly*. Perhaps most importantly, they practice a degree of fluidity—as though cross-training, they leverage what they learn in one arena and apply it to others. They use their portraiture, Ashtanga yoga, or dirt-bike racing experience to make them more creative scientists, business leaders, or nonfiction authors (and vice versa).

It's for this reason that I urge you to learn and explore your world like a fox. Pursue a wide range of goals, and resist the pressure to bury what makes you interesting. Don't be shy about your past, your failures, or your humor. If people judge you because you're not a hedgehog, they're not seeing the big picture. I can say with confidence that the things I pursued, explored, and endured outside the scope of my profession broadened my perspective and forced me to grow far more than pretty much any professional experience. I find this so valuable, in fact, that when hiring, I've always been wary of hedgehogs, even for highly specialized roles. To quote business mogul Kevin O'Leary, "Business is binary—you either make money or lose money; art is chaos. Good business leaders dip into art to solve business problems."

Actually, perhaps professional weirdo Vincent Price put it a bit more simply when he said, "A man who limits his interests limits his life."

It Sounds Cheesy, but Gratitude Matters

Someone once told me that his life changed when he began more actively *practicing gratitude*. I admit that I thought it seemed cheesy. I suppose I always thought *practicing gratitude* meant standing across from someone while wearing some sort of hemp shawl, putting my hands on their shoulders, locking eyes intensely, and saying something like, "My soul acknowledges all you've given me," leaving the recipient feeling indescribably awkward.

As I traversed the phases of my life, however, I came to understand that *practicing gratitude* doesn't necessarily mean addressing anyone directly or even expressing gratitude outwardly; rather, it means that there's value in simply dedicating occasional time and energy to appreciating the roles different individuals have played or continue to play in your life. This practice changes you in subtle ways that bleed into almost everything you do. It's taught me the art of patience, trained me to better articulate both appreciation and criticism, and forced me to consider others' perspectives and experiences more deeply.

Maybe it *is* a little cheesy, but it's still valid.

I urge you to take a few minutes now and then to be intentionally grateful to the bosses who took a chance on you and the customers who supported your business, even if some of them were assholes. I urge you to be grateful for the individuals who appreciate your vision as an artistic or creative force, and ask that you never take them for granted, no matter how much success you may experience. I urge you to be grateful for those who held you accountable as you pursued your goals, and to recognize that it may have been uncomfortable for them to do so.

With that said, I'll close this book with an expression of gratitude. Over the course of my professional life, I've worn many hats and been many things to many people, but helping people develop and adopt the **Values, Language, Behaviors**, and **Traditions** needed to execute on the things that really matter to them has, by far, been the most fulfilling thing I've ever had the privilege of doing. I couldn't experience that fulfillment without you and others taking the time to engage with my work and embrace my message. I hope you enjoyed this book, and I thank you from the bottom of my heart for giving it a chance. My only request is that you pass it on to someone you think could find it valuable.

Now, go. I could tell you to stay inspired. To stay motivated, to exercise self-discipline, and to love yourself—and that if you do so, everything will fall into place. But you know I won't because that would be bullshit. Instead, I'll convey a *much-less-sexy-but-much-more-pragmatic* message: I'll urge you to remain organized and meticulous. I'll urge you to remain honest and accountable. I'll urge you to remind yourself daily that execution is never the result of a series of hopes and wishes, and that it's instead the result of consistently applying the **Values**, **Language**, **Behaviors**, and **Traditions** you just learned. If you follow them, you'll be the author of your own fate in a very direct and tangible way.

Lastly, I'll urge you to *never*—under any circumstances—trust yourself at *Points B, C,* and beyond; those people are going to ruin your life over and over again unless you consistently take steps to outmaneuver them. They're the enemy. *Human against self.*

KEY TERMS AND CONCEPTS

Accountability   Sharing goals, **Mile Markers**, **CMVs**, or other aspects of your intentions with other individuals so they can follow along with your progress, failures, and inaction.

Agility   The ability and willingness to adjust to unexpected changes.

Appropriate Agility   The practice of exercising **Agility** without using it as an excuse to give up or change your goal in a way that violates your **CMV**.

Auditor   An individual tasked with ensuring that the **Executor of Consequences** follows through on their duties; a secondary layer of **Accountability** that helps see that **Tactical Consequences** are carried out when—by nature—they require third-party assistance.

Behaviors   The things you do due to your involvement with a **Culture**. **Behaviors**

are one of the four core aspects of a
Culture.

Blocked Time

Time dedicated to advancing a specific
goal, work track, or undertaking.

**Building a Body of
Work**

The process of accruing credibility,
wisdom, networks, and experience for the
sake of serving an eventual ambitious
goal.

Calendar

An **Execution Tool** used to organize not
only your commitments, but also sessions
of **Blocked Time** relating to your **Have-
to-Dos** and goals/**Want-to-Dos**.

CMV

An acronym which stands for **Credo,
Mission**, and **Vision**; all three play
important roles in defining your goal.

Credo

Beliefs about what's valuable, important,
or desirable. A **Credo** is one of the three
aspects of a **CMV** and should begin with
the words, "I believe…"

Culture

The **Behaviors, Values, Traditions**, and
Language associated with a group of one
or more individuals.

Daily Script	A **Script** specifically dedicated to outlining a consistent repeated daily process, such as what one does when first waking, going to bed, or first arriving at work or school.
Domain of Control	The set of factors and **Behaviors** that you can directly affect or influence (without relying on third parties) in pursuing a goal.
Dream	A goal that lacks clear criteria for achievement or a plan of action.
Execution Tools	The **Notebook**, **Listing Tool**, and **Calendar** you use to organize both complex goals and your life, in general.
Executor of Consequences	An individual tasked with enforcing the **Tactical Consequences** tied to your goal's **Mile Markers** when—by nature—your **Tactical Consequences** require third-party assistance.
Exploratory Phase	A period of dedicated research during which you work to become intimately familiar with a goal in every way possible.

Flight Club	A group of (ideally) four individuals who meet monthly in order to provide **Accountability** and insight to one another in a structured manner.
Focus Rhythms	Your personal thresholds for attention and mental fatigue, and the cadence derived from these thresholds, balancing time spent actively working on an endeavor versus time spent clearing your mind.
Foundational Success	A strong equity position in the currency you value at the deepest level (**Foundational Wealth**).
Foundational Wealth	The currency—whether experiences, material possessions, sensations, or anything else—that you value at the deepest level.
Foundations of Execution	The three **Behaviors** that typically set apart those who consistently execute on their goals from those who consistently fail to do so; the fundamental principles from which this entire book's core concepts are derived.
The Franklin Principle	The idea that meticulously organizing the things that you *have to do* lets you

maximize uninterrupted time with which you can guiltlessly do what you *want to do*.

Goal Scaffold	A nested list of **Major** and actionable **Minor Tasks** that come about from dissecting a goal; a step-by-step instruction manual detailing every step you need to take from your initial (or current) state in order to execute on your goal.
Have-to-Do	Something you need to do, although you may not necessarily enjoy or even find value in doing it.
Hierarchical Thought	Categorizing and placing people, places, ideas, things, and time within hierarchies as a means by which to manage complexity.
Hot List	A dynamic, prioritized, and up-to-date list of the things you're actively working on relating to a specific goal, work track, or undertaking; it should contain both *to-do*-style items and items to which you need to continue paying ongoing attention.

Inappropriate Agility	The practice of using **Agility** as an excuse to give up or change your goal in a way that violates your **CMV**.
Incoming Interruption	Interruption and distraction from external sources, such as other individuals, technology (push notifications), media, etc.
Intentionality	Performing a task or tasks with purpose (as opposed to simply *performing them*).
Language	The terms you use that are unique to your **Culture**. **Language** is one of the four core aspects of a **Culture**.
Listing Tool	An **Execution Tool** used to create and maintain your **Hot Lists**, **Goal Scaffolds**, and **Scripts**, as well as any dynamic information.
M-SMART Goal	A goal that is Motivation-focused, Specific, Measurable, Attainable, Realistic, and Time-Bound.
Major Task	A task in a **Goal Scaffold** that isn't necessarily independently actionable, and which is comprised of one or more **Minor Tasks**.

Mile Markers	Tasks that serve as checkpoints of achievement signifying progress toward executing on a goal.
Minor Task	A task in a **Goal Scaffold** that's independently actionable; one or more **Minor Tasks** can exist as components of a single **Major Task**.
Mission	Your purpose or calling; a manifestation of your **Credo**. A **Mission** is one of the three aspects of a **CMV** and should begin with the word, "To…"
Note-Taking Tool	An **Execution Tool** used to create and maintain long or multimedia content.
Outgoing Interruption	Interruption and distraction that you yourself initiate, such as engaging with other individuals, technology, media, etc.
Personal Culture	A **Culture** that begins and ends with you. The **Behaviors**, **Values**, **Traditions**, and **Language** you celebrate and those you don't tolerate; the way you communicate, what you eat, how you dress, the things that define you, the impression you make on others, and your own impression of yourself or your work.

Philosophy

One of the three perspectives through which you can address the three **Foundations of Execution** (or any complex or multifaceted concept); **Philosophy** refers to the broad idea or reasoning behind the concept.

Priority

The recognition that some tasks need to be completed before others due to factors like deadlines, financial considerations, and risk.

Recurring Task

A task, event, or **Behavior** that occurs more than once or on a consistent or regular basis.

Script

A simple, static, ordered process you follow to keep yourself on task when it's time to work on a goal, work track, or undertaking.

SMART Goal

A goal that's Specific, Measurable, Attainable, Realistic, and Time-Bound. The concept of a **SMART Goal** has existed for decades and, unlike **M-SMART Goals**, aren't unique to **Foundations of Execution**.

Strategy

One of the three perspectives through which you can address the three

Foundations of Execution (or any complex or multifaceted concept); **Strategy** refers to the ways in which you implement the concept's **Philosophy.**

Tactical Consequences

Specific distressing experiences that can result from failing to execute on goals, or—ideally—**Mile Markers** related to goals.

Tactics

One of the three perspectives through which you can address the three **Foundations of Execution** (or any complex or multifaceted concept); **Tactics** refer to the detailed, granular actions you take to implement the **Strategy**.

Test Case

A description of an event that can only successfully take place when a task has been satisfactorily completed.

Time Currency

The perspective that time is a unique form of true global currency; that you can't create it or accrue more of it, and that in spending it, you'll in every case be left with less of it.

Time Management

Performing tasks in a certain way, in a certain order, and at certain times or within certain time frames, in order to get more done in a shorter amount of time, or something of that nature.

Traditions Actions and stories that paint a picture of your **Values**. **Traditions** are one of the four core aspects of a **Culture**.

Unique Task A task, event, or **Behavior** that occurs only once.

Values The things you feel are important. **Values** are one of the four core aspects of a **Culture**.

Vision An image of a goal's **Mission** accomplished or being accomplished. A **Vision** is one of the three aspects of a **CMV**.

Want-to-Do Something you enjoy or find value in doing.

Made in the USA
San Bernardino,
CA